Design-It-Yourself
Clothes

Published in the United States by Potter Craft, an imprint of the Crown Publishing Group,

a division of Random House, Inc., New York.

www.crownpublishing.com

www.pottercraft.com

POTTER CRAFT and colophon is a registered trademark of Random House, Inc.

Library of Congress Cataloging-in-Publication Data

Patch, Cal.

Design-it-yourself clothes : patternmaking simplified / Cal Patch.—1st ed.

p.   cm.

Includes bibliographical references and index.

ISBN 978-0-307-45139-2 (alk. paper)

1. Dressmaking—Pattern design.   I. Title.

TT520.P322   2009

646.4'072-dc22

2008050344

Printed in China

Design by Kara Plikaitis

Photography by Heather Weston

Illustrations by Cal Patch & Frances Soohoo

10   9   8   7   6   5   4   3

First Edition

Design-It-Yourself
Clothes

Patternmaking Simplified

Cal Patch

POTTER
CRAFT

New York

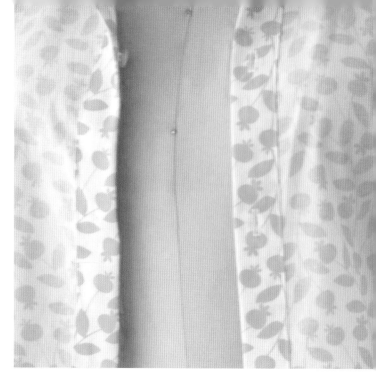

Introduction

WHY PATTERNMAKING?

PICTURE THIS: You're out shopping, maybe at your favorite vintage shop, maybe at a fancy designer boutique, and you see something familiar. Hmm. Where have you seen that dress before, you wonder. *In a magazine? A movie?* Oh wait, you remember! You've seen it *in your dreams!*

You try it on, and for a moment, you are enraptured: Life is complete! You will forevermore be the one envied at every party for what you are *wearing*. But then you do a reality check. The color, now that you are thinking clearly, doesn't suit you at all. The fabric is a little more synthetic than you'd like. The waist is actually too small, and wouldn't it be way dreamier with a wider, kimono-esque sleeve? And a different neckline? Not to mention longer, with more flare at the hemline, and some shirring at the bust? And again, you realize, this scenario is all too familiar: You know exactly what you want, and you've got the sewing skills to pull it off, if only there weren't that one, teensy-weensy recurring problem: the pattern. Even the best seamstress needs one, but a pattern for the vision in your head just plain does not exist. Yet.

It's no secret that sewing is the new hot craft—more people are –sewing now than ever before. Sooner or later, most stitchers want to tackle more advanced projects, namely clothing. This is where the trouble sets in. The problem isn't in the sewing, but in the pattern. Unfortunately, finding the perfect pattern for what you want to make can be anywhere from difficult to impossible. The sewing pattern industry, with a few noteworthy exceptions, doesn't seem to be quite in sync with the surge in modern sewers—sewers who want to make clothes that look like what they might buy at their favorite retailers.

The new generation of indie seamstresses is watching *Project Runway*, reading *ReadyMade* and *Selvedge*, and shopping at small boutiques selling one-offs by local designers. You know what you want to wear but can't always find it on a rack. You know how to sew but don't see patterns that resemble what you want to make. You *do* want to make a unique look based on your own personal taste, influences, and body type. And you need the freedom to create patterns as your taste evolves over time. What's an intrepid stitcher to do?

Well, the obvious answer is to learn how to make your own sewing patterns! Patternmaking is an age-old art form, which, at its core, is extremely simple. The clothing we currently wear tends to be relatively simple from a patternmaker's point of view. We don't wear finely tailored suits or dresses with princess seams, darts, and gussets. We wear simple knit tops, skirts, loose dresses, basic woven shirts, and pants. Their style tends to come from details, as opposed to dramatic or complicated cut and construction. Thus, it's quite possible to teach today's sewers how to make their own patterns. And this book does just that in a fun, concise volume for the modern girl.

There are other reasons, besides the lack of selection, to learn how to make patterns. For example, three little letters: F-I-T. Fit can make or break a look. Whether shopping for clothing or patterns, finding

ones that fit is frequently a struggle. This is because clothing manufacturers can't possibly make clothes to fit every conceivable body height, width, shape, and every combination of those factors. So they aim for the middle ground and hope for the best. Commercial sewing patterns have the same problem, though they do offer the possibility of simple adjustments, like altering length or combining two sizes in different areas to approximate your body. But only building a pattern from scratch, around your own personal set of numbers, can ultimately result in a garment that fits like it was *made* for you. Because it was!

A final reason to make your own patterns is your own unique personal taste and style. It's pretty challenging to develop a completely original look if you're limited to what you can find at the local mall. Vintage is an option, but good luck finding just the "right" piece that also happens to a) be in decent condition, b) be affordable, and c) oh yeah, *fit* you! Independent designers can be a fantastic resource if you can find one who answers to the same muse you do, and if you can afford their wares. But if you long to stand out from the crowd in a way that you've never seen expressed before, it could be quite a wait before you see your dreams hanging on any rack. As a designer myself, I relate to this scenario more than any other, and you have my sincere sympathies. But before we cue the music for our pity party, I've got some news for you: The wait is *over*. You can actually make the clothes you see in your head—you've just got some learning to do. But it's going to be fun, I promise!

In this book we are going to take the problem of sewing patterns into our own hands. I have organized it like a course in patternmaking, so you'll learn basic principles first, and then build on them in successive projects. You will get the most out of this book if you tackle the projects in order, but if you decide (as we're all inclined) to skip around, just be aware that you may occasionally need to backtrack a bit for certain projects. But whether you choose the straight path or the meandering one, it's going to be a wonderful journey! We'll discuss the tools used in patternmaking and the importance of selecting the right fabric for every garment. You'll learn how to take your own unique set of measurements, all of which add up to a map of *your* body, which is not the same as anyone else's. You will learn how to use those measurements to draft basic patterns for an A-line skirt, a T-shirt, a button-down shirt, pants, and a dress. With simple add-ons like pockets, trims, or ruffles, these five patterns alone could build an entire wardrobe and keep your sewing machine humming for years, but they're merely the beginning! Following each "basic" pattern lesson, you will find two variation projects, in which you'll alter a copy of the basic pattern to create more detailed versions. Once you've got these drafting skills down, I'll show you some of the methods for manipulating the foundation patterns even more to fulfill your inner designer's vision. We'll add stylized seams, flare, gathering, pleats and tucks, pockets, collars—just about anything you can dream up. Can you believe it? Let's get going!

Basic Dress
p. 92

Betsy Jacket

p. 83

—

Phoebe Skirt

p. 119

+ 9

Miette Dress
p. 98

Basic T
p. 58

—

Rosie Skirt
p. 49

Marguerite T
p. 66

—

Annie Trousers
p. 109

Charlotte Top
p. 69

—

Basic Skirt
p. 40

13

Gertie Dress
p. 97

Stella Blouse
p. 86

—

Laura Skirt
p. 46

15

Kathy Dress
p. 131

Basic T
p. 58

—

Olivia Knickers
p. 112

Sofie T
p.129

Carla Palazzo
p. 123

Miho Shirt
p.126

—

Basic Pant
p.104

Basic Shirt
p. 76

21

Part 1

BEFORE YOU BEGIN

Preparing to Make the Patterns

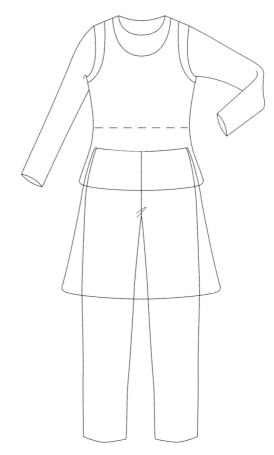

sketch template

Before we get started, I want to take a moment to give you an overview of the basic process of patternmaking. It probably still seems very mysterious at this point! In reality, though, it's a very practical art, as you will soon see. You'll begin by dreaming up some fantastical garment in your head that you would like to bring into this dimension. It's important to really clarify your vision, as you may never have realized before just how many parts, or **design elements**, there are in every garment. Even the simplest T-shirt has a neckline shape (scoop, V-neck, polo), neck edge finish (band, **binding**, **facing**), sleeve shape (straight, bell, wide), cuff finish (binding, cuff, turned back), hemline (straight, shirttail, **slits**), armhole (standard, raglan, dolman), fit (shrunken or oversized), length (cropped, tunic) and **silhouette** (A-line, fit-and-flare, boxy), not to mention fabric and color choices. Every one of these design elements was a choice made by someone.

Note: **As a kindness to you, the reader, sewing and pattern-making terms set in boldface throughout this book are defined in the Glossary (page 152).**

Also, in all cases I've used English, or Imperial, measurements throughout these patterns (that is, inches, feet, yards, etc.). For those who prefer metric measurements, a table of conversion ratios is included at the back of the book (page 157).

At first, you should definitely keep it simple while you're absorbing the new concepts. As you progress, you'll be able to get more fancy. Remember, my goal for this beginner book is to teach you how to make simple, modern clothes, not elaborate gowns or costumes. If you take a look in your closet, you'll see that most of the clothes you wear are versions of the same basic styles; the variation is mainly in the details. So, choose a design, and make a quick sketch of it. OK, a lot of you are probably freaking out about now because you think you can't draw, but remain calm. The sketch doesn't have to be a

work of art; it just needs to be specific. I know you can fake it well enough to show the difference between a high round neck and a low V. You can even use the sketch template above under your paper as a guide. Just do it! No one but you ever has to see the sketch, but it will help you visualize what you're going for.

Now you can measure your body (or the body of whomever you're designing for) in the areas that the garment will cover, usually either the top or bottom half. With these measurements, you can begin plotting the pattern on paper. You'll draft the shape using a combination of actual body measurements and design choices. Sometimes you will have to guess, or hold the tape measure up to yourself in front of a mirror to help you visualize how the measurements relate to your body. It takes a bit of experience to be able to translate the curves and contours of your 3-D self onto a 2-D piece of paper, but trust me, it'll come!

Once you feel that your pattern is correct, or at least the best educated guess you can manage, you will cut out a first sample, which is commonly referred to as a **muslin**. This will be the first "test" of your pattern. It is extremely important that the fabric you use for any muslin (which may or may not be the **fabric** that is actually called **muslin***) behaves like the *fabric* you intend to use for the final garment. Always use a woven fabric for the muslin of a woven garment, and likewise use a knit muslin substitute for a knit garment. Only the seams of the muslin are **basted**; details like pockets and edge finishes are usually skipped, though certain elements (like collars and cuffs) may be included so that you can see how they look. The muslin is then tried on by the model, and fit and styling adjustments are made. Then the muslin can be taken apart and the corrections transferred onto the paper pattern piece. If necessary, a second (third, fourth . . .) muslin may be sewn, incorporating the corrections, and the process repeated until the pattern can be called "final." At this point, the pattern can be used as it is, or copied onto a harder cardboard to withstand repeated use. Instead of being held down with pins, **hard patterns** are held down with weights and traced with **tailor's chalk** or **wax** onto the fabric. Then the pattern is removed and the pieces are cut.

So that's the basic patternmaking process. Obviously, there are many ways to carry out each step and still arrive at the same end result, and you will develop your own methods and preferences as you begin making your own patterns. But the general plan will always involve an idea, measurements, drafting, making a muslin, fitting, and correcting.

Gathering the Goods

Before you can begin to learn patternmaking, you will need a few basic supplies. Having taught classes for nearly a decade, I firmly believe that the best way to learn is by *doing*. If you try to read some of the chapters in this book before you're prepared to start, you'll quickly see that it's hard to make sense of what I'm saying if you're not doing it along with me, step by step. That said, the only ultimately essential supplies you need to make patterns are paper, a pencil, some scissors, and a ruler, and you probably have all of these items lying around your house. If so, you can get started immediately and upgrade to better versions of these tools later on, once

you see how much fun you're having! I'm not a fan of investing a whole lot of money into a new skill before I'm sure I'm going to stick with it, so I'll offer suggestions about ways to find alternative supplies that won't break the bank. The good news, though, is that there really aren't that many tools you'll need, even once you're ready to commit. I'll talk about each of the required supplies individually, starting with what you can find without investing a small fortune, and continuing on to the "professional" versions that will make your life easier.

NECESSARY TOOLS

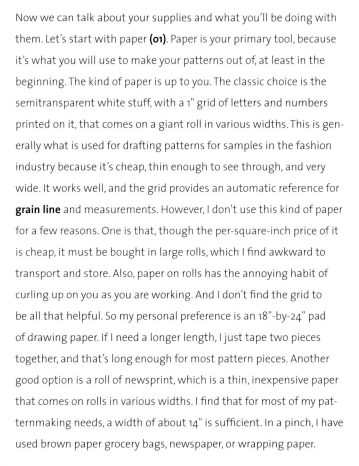

Now we can talk about your supplies and what you'll be doing with them. Let's start with paper **(01)**. Paper is your primary tool, because it's what you will use to make your patterns out of, at least in the beginning. The kind of paper is up to you. The classic choice is the semitransparent white stuff, with a 1" grid of letters and numbers printed on it, that comes on a giant roll in various widths. This is generally what is used for drafting patterns for samples in the fashion industry because it's cheap, thin enough to see through, and very wide. It works well, and the grid provides an automatic reference for **grain line** and measurements. However, I don't use this kind of paper for a few reasons. One is that, though the per-square-inch price of it is cheap, it must be bought in large rolls, which I find awkward to transport and store. Also, paper on rolls has the annoying habit of curling up on you as you are working. And I don't find the grid to be all that helpful. So my personal preference is an 18"-by-24" pad of drawing paper. If I need a longer length, I just tape two pieces together, and that's long enough for most pattern pieces. Another good option is a roll of newsprint, which is a thin, inexpensive paper that comes on rolls in various widths. I find that for most of my patternmaking needs, a width of about 14" is sufficient. In a pinch, I have used brown paper grocery bags, newspaper, or wrapping paper.

The second item you'll need is a good old-fashioned pencil **(02)**. You'll also need an eraser and a pencil sharpener, for obvious reasons. If you prefer a mechanical pencil, that's fine. Once your patterns are final, you may wish to trace over your lines in ink to make them more visible and permanent. But for the drafting and correcting stages, you'll be doing lots of erasing and re-drawing, so a pencil is your marking tool of choice.

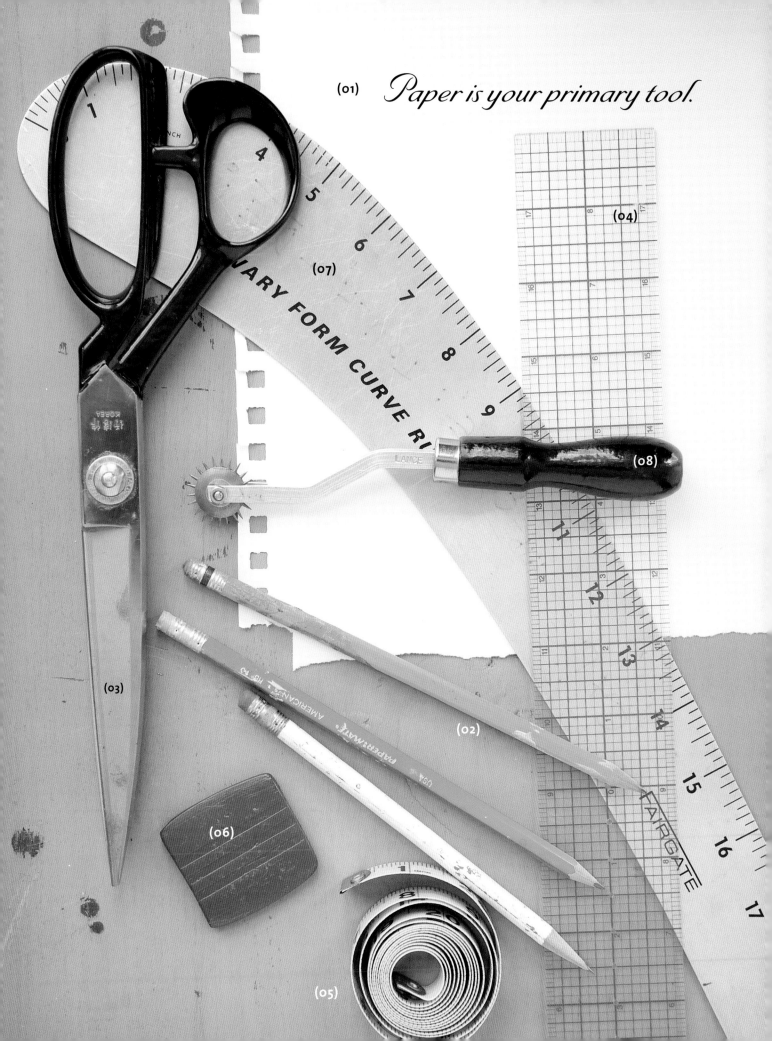

(01) *Paper is your primary tool.*

You will also need a good, sharp pair of scissors **(03)**. Since I'm assuming that you sew, you probably have a nice pair of sewing shears, and you've been told never to cut paper with them. Don't! Cutting paper with them will dull the blade and they won't cut fabric anymore. You probably also have a pair of old household scissors in your kitchen drawer, the ones that convinced you to buy the shears when you tried to use them to cut fabric for the first time. Those won't work either. Get yourself a decent pair of scissors and label them "for paper only." They don't need to be expensive; they just need to make a nice, clean cut. A good, economical brand is Fiskars, which makes an infinite number of styles.

The last tool you'll need in order to get started is a ruler. You can get by temporarily with a basic plastic or metal ruler, or even a yardstick. But a 2"-wide, 18"-long, clear plastic flexible sewing ruler **(04)** is the one tool I strongly recommend you buy once you start making patterns. It comes in handy for sewing too, so you'll always have a use for it. My favorite is the Quilt and Sew ruler by Collins (the original, without the metal edge), because the grid extends straight across the full 2" width of the ruler. This type of ruler is advantageous because of its built-in squaring function; as you'll soon see, squaring is a technique that you will use all the time in patternmaking. Since the grid extends across the entire ruler, you'll have a good 2" line to use for squaring, whereas the rulers that include centimeters on one side only give you a 1"-wide grid. And besides, sewing and patternmaking (at least in the United States) are firmly entrenched in the English system of measurement. Another useful feature of this ruler is that it's flexible, so it can be used to measure curved lines, or as a guide for drawing customized curves.

With those four items, you can get pretty far into patternmaking. They really are the only absolutely essential tools you couldn't function without. There are also a bunch of common household or sewing supplies that you will find yourself needing again and again for patternmaking, so you may want to gather an extra set so that everything you need can be kept in one place. These include a tape measure **(05)**, transparent tape, safety pins, tailor's chalk or wax **(06)**, **dressmaker's carbon paper**, and a stapler. Most of the additional supplies I'll suggest are mainly to make your life easier and save time as you work.

OPTIONAL TOOLS

On that note, at the top of the list of optional tools is the **hip curve (07)**, sometimes also called a "fashion ruler." This is a type of ruler used for drawing curved lines, part of a whole category of **curve rulers**, which includes **French curves** as well. The hip curve is one that is specifically designed for use in garment patternmaking. My preference is the Vary Form Curve Rule by Fairgate. It has a nice, gently increasing curve that is very helpful in determining hip, armhole, and neckline curves. However, let me give you the disclaimer I give to my students with regard to curve rulers: Just because your hip curve was designed to correspond to certain common curves found on patterns, it does not mean that it will always automatically provide you with the perfect curve for your every need. Only you, the designer, can truly determine the correct curve. So use any type of curve ruler as a guide or helper, not as a master!

Once you've made a pattern, you'll need muslin. There are two different, but closely related, meanings for this term. One refers to the inexpensive, unbleached cotton woven fabric that is traditionally used for making first samples, or **prototypes**. The second is the prototype itself. Essentially, the purpose of a muslin is to make any corrections/adjustments/improvements to the pattern before you cut into your precious, possibly expensive, maybe even irreplaceable final fabric, to avoid wasting it. The fabric called muslin is a fine choice for your sample, as long as you'll be using a lightweight woven fabric for your final garment. We'll talk more about muslin in the section on fitting.

Another item you may want to try out is card stock or **oak tag**. These heavier papers are used in the industry to make hard patterns. If you plan to only use your pattern once or twice, or if you're not sure yet how many times you'll use it, don't bother making a hard pattern just yet. But if you have big plans to make multiples of something to sell or give as gifts, hard patterns can save you much time in the long run because they are so much easier to use. Professional patternmaking-quality oak tag comes in sheets or rolls. A cheap alternative, if you just want to test out the idea, is to get poster board at your neighborhood drugstore or office/art supply store. Here's how you do it: Once you have tested out your pattern with a muslin and made corrections to the original, trace each piece onto one of these lightweight cardboards, copy all markings onto the new pieces, and cut them out. To use them, lay the pieces out on your fabric just as with a paper pattern, but instead of pinning the pieces down, hold them in place with weights (I usually use cans of soup, water bottles, or anything I have nearby), and trace around the pattern with tailor's chalk/wax or a marking pen. Then remove the pattern pieces and cut right into your fabric. This method works great if you are stacking multiple layers of fabric to cut all at once, as it's not easy to pin through too many layers.

While we're on the subject, I should mention that there are actual, officially sanctioned patternmaker's weights. They're big, clunky things, reminiscent of old-fashioned irons. I personally have never felt a need to invest in these, but you may feel differently! Or you may inherit some, or come across them at a flea market, so it's good to know they exist. I've also seen a new, smaller type of weight (one brand is Wonder Weights) that does look very useful and much more compact than the traditional kind. Still, I find that it's pretty easy to just grab the nearest heavy objects (cans, rocks, scissors . . .) whenever I need a weight!

Pushpins are a handy tool for holding garments in place as you trace or "rub" a pattern off them. They are the thumbtacks with the bigger plastic or metal tops, which make them much easier to grasp than the flat kind. Pushpins are also used to transfer points or lines from one pattern piece onto another piece of paper, in making another pattern piece. But I'll explain more about that when we get there.

If you get serious about making patterns, you might want to get a needle-point **tracing wheel (o8)**. You might already have the kind of tracing wheel with the zigzag edge, used with dressmaker's carbon, but the one that patternmakers use has needle points extending from the wheel, for transferring a line of holes through a garment or pattern and into your paper.

It is helpful to have a cutting mat to use as your work surface when you are using push pins or a tracing wheel, as you may not want to poke holes in your dining room table or whatever surface you'll be using to make your patterns. Since I use a large pad of drawing paper as my patternmaking paper, the cardboard at the back of the pad often becomes my convenient hole-poking mat.

- -

Labeling Patterns

It is very important to label every pattern piece you make with several bits of key information. First and foremost is the grain line. For most patterns it will be parallel to Center Front/Center Back, but you might occasionally want **bias** or **cross grain**, so the line should reflect whichever grain you choose. Differentiate the grain line from all other lines by adding arrowheads to it. Once I have drawn a grain line, I write the following info on this line:

Name of style: Basic T, Long Ruffle Skirt, Gertie Dress— whatever you want to call the style should be on every pattern piece that pertains to it.

Name of pattern piece: Front Bodice, Cuff, Back Yoke—you get the idea.

Size or key measurements: I write the measurements I used to draft the pattern right on it, for reference later.

Cutting instructions: How many to cut, and if specific placement is required, like "Cut one on fold."

Any other pertinent information (size of seam allowance, "cut 1 in interfacing") you want to include can't hurt. Any notes ("Borrow sleeve from Stella Blouse" or "cut bias strip 18" x 2" for neck binding") should be written on the primary piece (usually the front). CF or CB should always be labeled, dart legs should be **notched**, dart points should be prominent and clear, any points where the piece will be matched to a seam or other piece should be notched, and pocket placements should be marked. I also like to number the pieces and indicate the total number of pieces included in the pattern (such as "2 of 5"). It's really up to you what information you put on your pattern pieces, but as your library grows, you'll find that the more details you have, the better.

TAKING YOUR MEASUREMENTS

OK, so you've got your basic supplies in order, you've cleared some space on the kitchen table, and you're ready to get started. The whole point of learning to make your own patterns is to make the clothes you *want* to wear, and make them to fit *your* body. So we need to jot down your measurements as a starting point. You may want to designate a notebook or binder as your "patternmaking journal" so that you can keep all your measurements, notes, and inspirations in one place. If you're going to do this, it'll be worthwhile to spend the time to take all your measurements in advance. Or you may prefer to only take the ones you need for the pattern you're about to draft. Either way works. At the beginning of every project in this book, I'll list the measurements you'll need for that particular pattern. If you do make a master list of your measurements, keep in mind that they may change over time, so you'll need to update the list periodically. Following is a comprehensive list of what you'll need to measure and how to go about it. (The explanations starting on page 31 are presented in the order in which a pattern is drafted). Grab your tape measure and find yourself a full-length mirror; let's take some measurements!

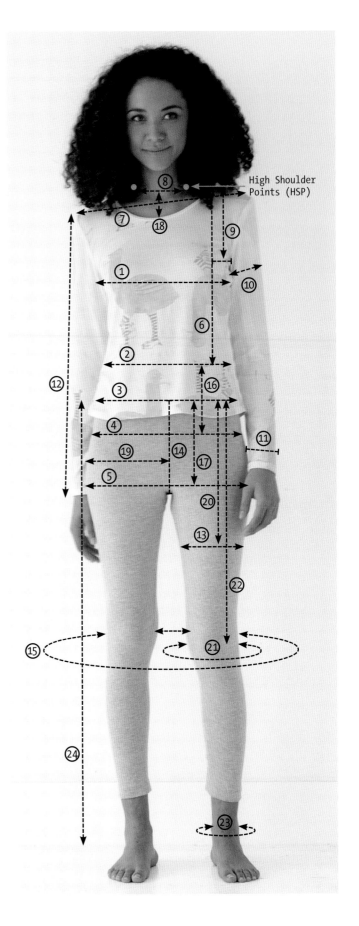

High Shoulder Points (HSP)

1. bust circumference
2. true waist circumference
3. low waist circumference
4. high hip circumference
5. low hip circumference
6. waist down from HSP
7. shoulder width
8. neck width
9. armhole height
10. bicep circumference
11. wrist circumference
12. sleeve length
13. thigh circumference
14. front rise height
15. sweep circumference
16. high hip down from (true) waist
17. low hip down from (low) waist
18. front neck drop
19. front hip
20. thigh down from waist
21. knee circumference
22. knee down from waist
23. (pant) cuff circumference
24. pant length

For Shirts, Dresses, and Skirts

Bust: To measure your bust, wrap the tape measure around your chest at its fullest point. Be sure that the loop you're making around yourself is roughly parallel to the floor, and that it's not dipping up or down as it wraps around you. This number should be the same as your bra size.

Waist: Believe it or not, the *waist* is a somewhat subjective term, which changes according to history and fashion. The traditional waist is the smallest part of you, generally just below your lowest rib. In recent years, however, we tend to wear our skirts and pants down around our hips instead of the **true waist**. You may want to have both measurements on hand, as the higher waist is helpful in shirts and dresses if you want a fitted look, and the lower one is what you'll use as the waist line for bottoms. You can call these *true waist* and *low waist* to avoid confusion. Generally the true waist will be used only for top patterns and the low waist for bottoms.

Waist down from HSP: HSP stands for **high shoulder point**, which is the point at which your neck meets your shoulder. This may or may not be a clear "point" on your body, so you'll just have to decide where it is and then be consistent. This is the point from which we measure the length of a garment, and from which we determine where to place our horizontal lines (bust line, waist line, etc.) in drafting our patterns. For this measurement, "waist down from HSP," you are measuring the distance from HSP to the imaginary line where you determined your waist measurement. If you are using both the true waist and the low waist, you'll need a "down from HSP" for each.

High hip: Traditionally, patternmakers use two hip measurements, a high one and a low one. The high one is where your hip bones are, but that is essentially where we wear our jeans and skirts today, so I refer to it instead as the *waist* or the *low waist*. However, if you prefer to use a more classic higher waistline, you may want to use this high hip measurement as well.

High hip down from waist: As with the waist down from HSP, this is the distance from your waistline (true waist) down to where you measured the high hip.

Low hip: This is the only hip measurement I use, and it's measured at your widest point. Your widest point may or may not correspond with anything you call "hips"; more likely it'll correspond to your "bum." Look in the mirror to help you determine your widest point, both straight-on and from the side. I know, it's not a number most of us want to take ownership of, but trust me, you'll need to know it!

Low hip down from waist: Wherever you determined that dreaded widest point to be, measure the distance between it and your waist. In this case I'd recommend using your low waist, as that's the one that'll be used for bottom (skirt and pant) patterns.

Shoulder width: For this one, look in the mirror while holding your tape measure straight across your shoulders, at the outermost ends of your collarbones (these are your shoulder points). This determines the placement of your armhole seams.

Neck width: Again, hold the tape measure straight across the front of your neck while looking in the mirror. Don't wrap it *around* your neck; the tape must remain flat. You'll have to do a little visualizing to get this measurement, but it's basically the distance between your two high shoulder points (HSPs), if you could draw a line straight between them, right through the middle of your neck.

Front neck drop: This one also requires a little vision. It's the distance from HSP to the bottom edge of your neckline at **Center Front** (the imaginary line that runs down the center of the body), but in a straight, vertical line. I usually hold my hand horizontally across my neck at the front points of my collarbones, then measure from HSP down to my hand. For now, just think of this as your *minimum* front **neck drop;** you can get all dramatic with the low scoop necks later!

Back neck drop: Same as front; just eyeball the highest point you'd ever make a back neckline. Generally it'll be ½" at the very least.

Armhole height: Place your left thumb at the front of your right armpit, and your left index finger at the back of it, so your hand makes a nice curve under the pit. Measure from your shoulder point down to the lowest part of this curve, in a straight line.

Bicep: Wrap the tape around your bicep at its fullest.

Wrist: Measure the circumference of your wrist, right where the wrist bone protrudes.

Sleeve length: Measure the distance from your shoulder point to your wrist bone, with arm straight.

Sweep: The official term for the circumference of a hem, generally used for skirts and dresses only. It's not actually a body measurement, but rather a design measurement. It is dependent on the length of the skirt or dress. There are, however, some considerations in reference to the body. For example, a miniskirt may have a sweep of 38", but if you use that same sweep on a floor-length dress, you won't be able to walk!

Front bodice height: In a dress, this refers to how long you want the upper part of dress (the **bodice**), usually from HSP to waist seam. For a strappy dress, the bodice height may not reach all the way to HSP.

Back bodice height: Meaure as above, only for the back.

For Pants Only

Front hip: For pants, it is important to distinguish the difference between the front and back sides of the lower torso, so the front hip is measured across, from (imaginary) side seam to side seam, at the hip line.

Back hip: As with front hip, this is measured from side to side across the back hip line.

Rise height: This is the distance from the waistline (top edge of pant) to the crotch, measured in a straight line. Wearing a pair of well-fitting pants, hold a ruler or book between your legs so that it touches the crotch seam of the pants. Measure from the top edge of the ruler or book to the intended waistline of the pant.

Thigh circumference: Measure loosely around the middle of your thigh, 3–4" below the crotch, with as much ease as you'd like to have in the pants.

Thigh down from waist: This is the distance from the waistline (top edge of pant) to the point at which you measured the thigh circumference.

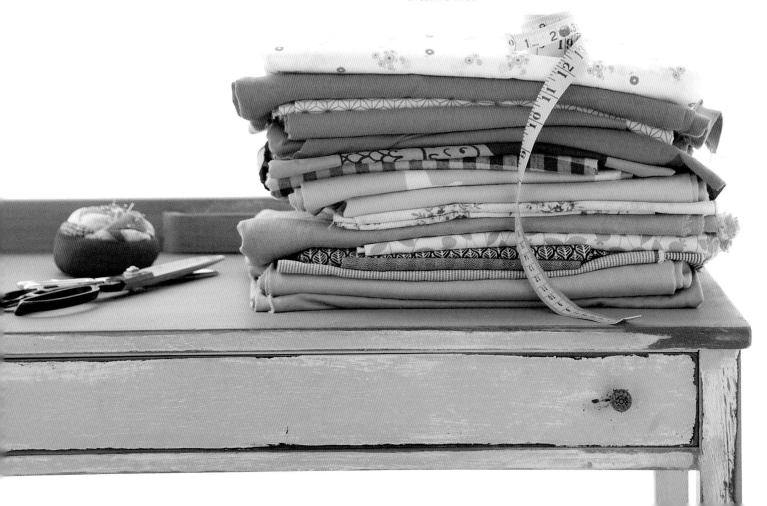

Knee circumference: As for the thigh, measure loosely around the knee. Remember that there must be ample room for your knee to move and bend! You are measuring how you want the pants to fit, not how big your actual knee is.

Knee down from waist: The distance from waistline to the point at which you measured the knee circumference.

Cuff circumference: Measure loosely around your ankle, visualizing how you want the pants to fit. This is the circumference you'd like for the bottom edge of your pant, at the cuff.

While taking your measurements, there are a few concepts you should keep in mind:

First, don't skimp! You'll only be cheating yourself out of the whole point of drafting your own patterns. Try to make your numbers as accurate as possible. In other words, don't pull the tape measure tightly around your waist until it gives you the number you remember from high school. You must be honest with yourself, or the clothes you make from your patterns won't fit any better than the ones you buy; in fact, they'll be even worse! And any area where a lot of bending or movement occurs (like, say, your hips) should be measured on the generous side. We will add **ease** as we make our

patterns, but if you start out using numbers that are too small, adding a touch of ease won't be enough to allow for the breathing, bending, eating, and sitting we do all day.

Second, there are two types of measurements you will need as you are making your patterns. The ones I've just outlined above are the actual body measurements that will form the foundation of your pattern. But other measurements can only be determined by your eye and the vision of the garment you have in your mind. When I am drafting patterns I always have a full-length mirror nearby, and I spend a lot of time standing in front of it, holding the tape measure up to some part of me, trying to guesstimate measurements that will define the design of the garment. A simple example of what I'm talking about is length. There is nothing you can specifically measure on your body to determine the length of a garment, except maybe a floor-length dress.

Now that you have your measurements down on paper, you have the building blocks you need to start drafting your very first sewing patterns. As in any kind of building, the numbers are the foundation of the plans. Your body determines the basic parameters of the patterns you'll draft, and your vision and imagination will provide the infinite style options. So let's make some patterns!

Part 2

MAKING THE PATTERNS

The A-Line Skirt

When you're creating a pattern for a garment of your own design, there are a few ways to go about it. First, you need a clear idea of what you want. Pictures from magazines or catalogs are a great source of inspiration and reference. Designers keep files of tearsheets (pages torn from magazines) as they develop a collection, to show every facet of the look they're going for: silhouette, fabric, details, drape, color, print, styling. If you have a vision in your head, it may be helpful to look for photos of similar garments so that you can consider options you hadn't thought of: Do you want a waistband? pockets? Should the skirt be in a crisp fabric that will stand away from your body, or a softer, drapier fabric that will cling to your curves? If you can, you may want to make a sketch of your vision.

The look of your final result will be the product of many combined factors, like proportion, fabrication, details, fit, and finishing. All of these relate directly to your pattern.

In making this skirt, you'll learn some of the principles used in patternmaking, then you'll continue to build on this foundation with future projects. The first thing to know is that patterns are usually made for only one **quadrant** (quarter) of the body. What I mean is that even though the skirt will obviously cover the whole circumference of you, the two pattern pieces will each be for only one quadrant (either the left front or the left back). For this project you are going to design two pattern pieces for the skirt: a front ("front skirt") and a back ("back skirt"). But remember that each of these will only be *half* of the side of the body you're addressing; that is, they are each a *quarter* of your body's measurements. Make sense? The idea is for each of the patterns you design, front and back, to be cut on a folded piece of fabric, so that once unfolded, the quarters will become halves and the skirt will cover the whole circumference of your lower body. Whew!

BASIC SKIRT

For our first project, we're going to make an A-line skirt, which is a simple and classic shape that flatters everyone. The exciting part is that *you* are now the designer! You'll decide if you want yours a little more straight, or with a whole lot of **flare**; if you want it to sit at your waistline or below your belly button; and if the hem should fall below your knee or high on your thigh. As far as fabric choice, any stable woven will do; try it in denim, corduroy, twill, or a cotton print like I used.

MEASUREMENTS

Length of skirt

Waist* (in this case, where you want this skirt to sit)

Hip* (at your widest point; may be lower than you think!)

Low hip down from waist

Sweep*

For each of these horizontal measurements, add 1" for ease, and divide that number by 4. These quarter measurements will be the ones you use for drafting the pattern. They will be referred to as quarter-waist, quarter-hip, quarter-sweep, etc.

A Note about Measurements

You may notice that in the five measurements required to make the skirt, three are actual body measurements, but two are *desired* measurements. To some degree you will be *guessing* these numbers and fine-tuning them later, once you've made your muslin and can try it on. To figure out a guesstimate for your skirt length, stand in front of your full-length mirror and hold the top of the tape measure where you want the top of the skirt. Let the rest of it fall to the floor and, without bending over, eyeball your desired length on the tape. Don't worry too much about getting it exactly right, as it'll be easy to adjust later, but if in doubt, err on the longer side. You can always trim it shorter, but never longer!

Now for the sweep: This one's a little trickier to determine. I'd start by checking your closet to see if you have a skirt similar to what you envision. If so, try it on and see how it compares to your dream sweep; at the very least it gives you a jumping-off point to work from. Another point of reference is your hip measurement. Generally an A-line skirt is wider at the bottom than the hip (hence the *A*), so you'll probably want to add a minimum of 4" to your full hip circumference as a starter. For the purpose of this project, I wouldn't go more than 12" bigger than your hip; more flare than that needs to be added in a way that we'll learn later. I usually take a guess at what my sweep should be, make the tape measure into a loop that measures my guess, then hold it around my knees at the approximate length I plan the skirt to be. Then I try to walk. At this point I look like a ridiculous hobbit, hunched over and hobbling around, but it shows me that I can walk (i.e., the sweep is big enough) and helps me visualize the proportion in the mirror.

make the front skirt

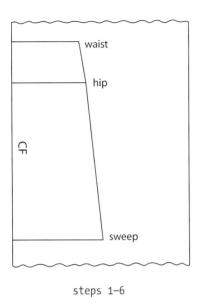

steps 1–6

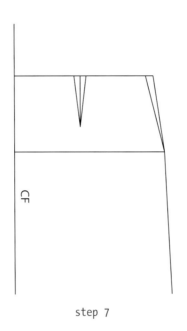

step 7

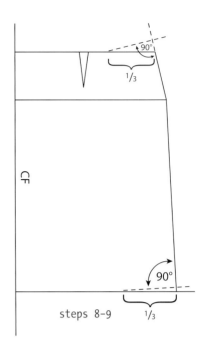

steps 8–9

Make the Front Skirt

1. Prepare your paper

Begin with a piece a piece of paper approximately 4" longer than the length of your skirt and at least 2" wider than your quarter-sweep. Make sure at least one of the long sides of the paper is a perfectly straight, smooth edge. If it isn't, draw a line with your ruler close to the edge, and cut on the line. All your drafting will begin from this edge, so it's important that it is straight and clean. Orient your paper so that this edge is on the left side. This edge will become Center Front (CF) on your skirt.

2. Plot the length

Along this left-side edge, make a small cross-mark about 2" down from the top edge of the paper. From this point, measure down the length of your skirt and make another mark there.

3. Plot the waist

At the top mark, align your clear ruler so that it intersects CF at a 90° angle (a.k.a. **perpendicular**). Draw a horizontal line here that measures your quarter-waist. This is your waist line. Make sure the end-

point of the line is clear; make a cross-mark or dot to define it.

4. Plot the sweep

At the bottom mark, draw another horizontal line, using your quarter-sweep measurement.

5. Plot the hip

Now, along CF, measure down from the waist line the distance from waist to hip, and make a cross-mark there. From this mark, plot a horizontal line that measures your quarter-hip.

6. Connect the dots

Draw a line from the endpoint of your waist line to the endpoint of your hip line, and from your hip line to the endpoint of your sweep line. This will become your **side seam**. Now you have a rough outline of your skirt pattern, though it probably looks like a pattern for a robot! Rest assured, we'll smooth out those corners to mimic your curvy self in a little while.

7. Make the darts

Next we'll add some darts so the waistline of your skirt won't only be shaped at the side

seams. Find the halfway point along your waist line, and mark it. This is where you're going to make the dart. From this halfway point, draw a line perpendicular to your waist (and parallel to CF) 3" down. Then, on the waist line, make a mark ¼" on each side of the dart line. Connect these two marks to the endpoint of your dart line 3" down. Now you have an upside-down triangle shape, a.k.a. your very first dart! See, this isn't so bad!

Note: This dart is ½" wide by 3" long, which is a fairly average front dart size. It may or may not, however, be just right for your body. This will be determined later when you try on the muslin, and adjust it accordingly. Trust me, I've got your back— I mean your front!

Now, you may be thinking that something feels funny here. How can we subtract ½" (¼" x 2) on each side of the skirt front (no telling yet *what's* going to happen on the back!) and have it still fit? I knew you were smart; I was just testing! We need to add back the ½" that we just pinched out, so extend your waist line by ½", and connect this *new* endpoint to your hip point. This new line is now the correct one; erase or

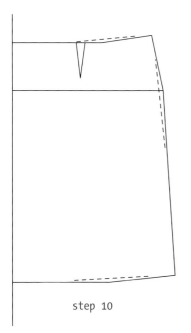

step 10

What's the Deal with Darts?

Darts are one of the unsung heroes of fit. Those funny little triangles on pattern pieces are where you'll pinch a little fullness out of a specific area, creating a subtle cone shape (so subtle it's more like a dome) where the fabric once laid flat. Darts help accommodate "cones of fullness" on your body, namely boobs and butts. To illustrate this concept, cut a circle (doesn't need to be perfect) out of a scrap of fabric or paper. Next cut a small piece out of the pie (don't be greedy!) and tape the two edges of the slice back together to close the gap. You'll see that the circle no longer lies flat; it's now a cone. That's how a dart gives a three-dimensional shape to a flat pattern piece. Cool, huh?

make little Xs on the old line so you won't get confused later.

8. SQUARE THE WAIST

OK, this is where we get radical. Squaring corners isn't hard, but if it does throw you for a loop, you won't be the first. It's actually quite simple, but it may take doing it a few times before it makes sense to you. Here's what I'm talking about: In general, all of our corners in patternmaking, where two seams will intersect, *must* be **right angles** (that's 90°). No biggie, right? But take a look at your pattern, and you'll see that the whole point to what we're doing here is to plot out the measurements of *your* body, so that the skirt fits you. And you, dear reader, are not a rectangle! Cue the curves: By bending our straight lines, we can make our corners **square**. Here's how you do it: Let's start at the waist. Sidle your ruler up along the side seam line, at the top of your pattern, and extend the side **seam line** up for 1". Now turn your ruler 90°, so that it is perpendicular to that extended side seam line. Slide it up and down that seam line (keeping the angle constant) until it intersects the waist line about one-third of the way over from the side seam

to CF (closer to the side seam). When you've hit the right spot, draw a line from the extended side seam to the waist line. This new line is correct, so as before, erase the old one or mark it with Xs.

9. SQUARE THE HEM

Repeat this process at the sweep line. Squaring the hem is almost the same as squaring the waist, except you will be slicing off the bottom corner instead of extending it. Hold your ruler perpendicular to the side seam, down near the sweep. Slide it up and down until the ruler intersects the sweep line one-third of the way over from the side seam to CF (closer to the side seam). Draw a line and erase the old one.

10. SMOOTH THE POINTS

All we need to do now is smooth out those angles to fit your fine human curves. Take your hip curve (or French curve) and lay it down alongside one of those pesky angles. (We're talking about the three **obtuse angles** now, *not* the 90° ones you just made. You should have one at the waist line, one at the hip point on your side seam, and one on your sweep line.) Slide the curve around until you find a

section of it that fits nicely into the angle. The edge of the hip curve should be *touching* your line at points a few inches to each side of the angle. Following the curve, draw a line between the two points. Erase or mark out the old lines. Repeat for the other 2 angles.

11. ADD SEAM ALLOWANCE

We'll be using ½" for our standard **seam allowance** (SA), but feel free to use ⅝" if you prefer. There are two ways to add SA. One is best for curves: Hold the ruler perpendicular to your seam line, and make a dot ½" out from the seam line. Now slide the ruler over a bit (maybe ½" or so), along the seam line, and repeat. Just be sure the ruler is always held exactly 90° to the seam. The more curvy the section of line, the closer together your dots should be. Then connect the dots into a smoothly curving line. On straighter sections, hold the ruler parallel to the seam line. Find the interior heavy line of the ruler that is ½" from the edge. Lay this line on top of your seam line, and draw along the edge of the ruler, only along the section where the seam line is lying directly under the ½" line on the ruler. Keep shifting the ruler to continue the SA along slight curves. Perfectly straight lines

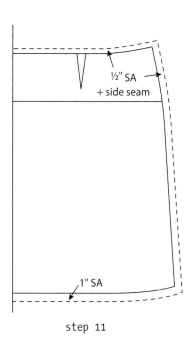

½" SA
+ side seam

1" SA

step 11

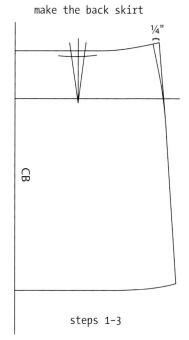

¼"

CB

steps 1–3

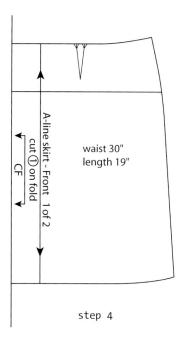

A-line skirt - Front 1 of 2

cut ① on fold

CF

waist 30"
length 19"

step 4

can be dealt with in one pass. With a little practice, you'll totally get the hang of it, I promise!

Tip: I like to add a full inch of SA along the bottom sweep, so I can do a ½" double-turned hem. Think about how you are likely to hem the skirt, and add your SA accordingly. But don't stress too much about it; you can always adjust later!

12. Check your work

Your first pattern piece is now basically done, but before you cut it out, let's just do a quick once-over.

* *Did you double-check that all four corners (CF waist, waist/side seam, sweep/side seam, and CF sweep) are right angles?*

* *Did you check that there aren't any other pointy bits aside from those four corners? They should have been smoothed out into curves just before adding the SA.*

* *Does the basic shape of the skirt look right to you? It should look pretty recognizable at this point, as half of a skirt that would fit*

you, so if anything looks really wacky, go back and check your measurements, and go over the steps again.

13. Fold dart and cut out

If everything checks out, there's one last tiny step before cutting, which is to fold your dart so that the two outer legs meet, and press the dart allowance toward the CF. Put a small piece of tape over the dart to hold it in place. *Now* you can cut out your pattern, cutting across the dart while it's folded (this will shape the edge of the dart allowance properly). Once it's all cut, you can remove the tape and unfold the dart.

Make the Back Skirt

1. Trace the front pattern

You'll need another piece of paper the same size as the one you began with, again with a long, straight edge along the left side. Lay your front pattern on top of the paper, aligning CF over the left side of the paper underneath. On this new pattern piece, the left edge signifies **Center Back** (CB). Trace around the front pattern so you'll have a replica of it on the new piece. Mark the center line of the dart at the waist line. Also mark the point

where the hip line meets the side seam. Set aside the front pattern.

2. Enlarge the dart

The main difference between the back skirt and the front is that the darts will be bigger, to allow for our curvier backsides. From the center point of the dart at the waist line, draw a vertical line (parallel to CB) 5½" down. This will make a 5" long dart, because our ½" SA is already added. At the waist, on each side of the center point, mark ⅜". Connect these two points down to the endpoint of the line you just drew. Now you have a ¾" wide (⅜" x 2) back dart.

3. Add back the difference

Any questions? Remember the test when we made the front? Here's your second chance to earn brownie points (mmm . . . brownies)! If this process is making sense to you, you should be noticing now that, in order for the skirt to fit, we'll need to add back what we just pinched out for the darts. The difference between our back dart and our front one is ¼", so that's what we need to add. (The back dart is ¾" wide, but we already added in ½" for the dart on the front, so we only need ¼"

more.) So hold your ruler along the waist line, right where it meets the side seam, and extend the waist line out for another ¼". Then connect this point with a straight line down to your hip point. This probably messes up your 90° angle, so **true** it up. Then smooth out that hip point. Your seam allowance is already in there, so all that's left is to fold and tape the dart and cut this baby out!

4. LABEL YOUR PATTERN PIECES

Label your pattern pieces with CF or CB, grain line, your style name, the name of each pattern piece (front skirt and back skirt), size or key measurements, and cutting instructions (front and back skirt pieces are "cut 1 on fold"). Extend your dart legs up to the SA line and notch them.

You did it! Now, if that accomplishment isn't a perfect excuse to bake a pan of brownies, I don't know what is. Just don't eat too many, or you'll have to re-draft your skirt!

SEWING INSTRUCTIONS: Stitch all darts. With right sides together, sew the right-side seam, using your choice of seam finish. Note: **Seams are generally always sewn with right sides together, except for French or flat-felled seams.** Insert a 7" invisible zipper at the top of left-side seam, then sew the lower end of the seam. Finish the waistline with an inside bias-tape facing. Hem your skirt using a double-turned ½" hem.

Adding a Waistband, Pockets, or a Ruffle

Now that you have your basic skirt pattern, you can add all sorts of bells and whistles to make variations on the original. One easy option is a waistband, and drafting one is a piece of cake! The pattern is going to be a long, skinny rectangle. To determine the length, use this formula: your full waist measurement (*not* the quarter-waist we used before) + 1" for ease + 1" overlap for a button closure + 1" for seam allowance (if you're using ½" SA) *or* 1¼" (if you're using ⅝" SA). To determine the width, figure out how wide you want the finished waistband to be, and double it. Take this number and add 1" *or* 1¼" for SA, as you did before. Voilà! There's your waistband pattern.

Another simple add-on is a patch pocket. For now let's stick with a rectangular one; you can get more creative later. Figure out how tall and wide you want the finished pocket to be.

Tip: To help you visualize this, cut out some samples using felt, and stick them on whatever you're wearing while looking in the mirror. The felt should stick to you without any pins. If you don't have any felt, a scrap of fabric or paper will work too; use pins or double-stick tape to try them on.

The length of your pocket pattern will be the length of your desired finished pocket + 1" for the top hem + ½" *or* ⅝" for the lower SA. The width will be the width of your finished pocket + 1" *or* 1¼" for SA. If you want, you can round off the lower corners, just fold the pattern in half (vertically) first so they'll be symmetrical. Be warned, though: Rounded corners may be cute, but they are tricky to turn!

A third option is to add a ruffle to the bottom of your skirt. Believe it or not, it's another rectangle! Take your full sweep measurement, and multiply it by 1.25 for a slightly gathered ruffle, 1.5 for a little more ruffliness, or double it for an all-out super ruffle. Add 1" *or* 1¼" SA. This will be the length of your pattern. For the width, figure out your desired ruffle width + ½" *or* ⅝" SA + 1" for the hem. OK, that should keep you busy for a while!

Skirt Variation 1: LAURA SKIRT

Now that you have begun building your pattern library, I'm going to show you how easy it is to take your basic patterns and alter them to create infinite style options. In this first variation, we'll add a **yoke** and ruffle to your Basic Skirt (page 40), for a modern prairie skirt Ms. Ingalls would have loved. My version is in a printed linen-like cotton, but you might use something softer like a gauze or voile. You'll need two pieces of paper, a bit bigger than your Basic Skirt patterns.

1. MAKE THE YOKE

Trace your front skirt pattern from page 42 onto one of the pieces of paper. Hold your ruler so it touches the bottom point of the dart, and swivel it around until you find the angle you like for your yoke seam. You will be drawing one straight line, from CF to the side seam, that touches the dart point along the way. Because we want a pointed yoke, this line will *not* meet CF at a 90° angle. Cut the pattern apart on this yoke seam line, and tape on a scrap of paper to add SA to the skirt piece. On the yoke piece, fold your dart closed and tape it shut. With your curve tool, smooth out the slight angle created by closing the dart; this line will be slightly curved, even though the corresponding seam line on the skirt is straight. The dart shaping will now be achieved by the yoke seam instead. Tape on a scrap of paper and add SA to the yoke seam line.

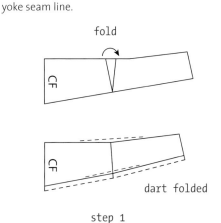

fold

dart folded

step 1

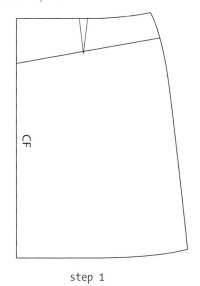

step 1

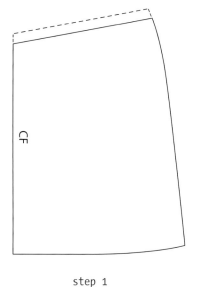

step 1

2. Make the back skirt

Repeat step 1 for the back skirt and yoke, being sure to have the back yoke meet the front at the side seams.

Note: In making the back yoke, it's fine to shave the bottom inch or so off the dart; just fold to the bottom of the yoke seam when you are eliminating the dart from the yoke piece. Check that the back and front pieces match at the side seams.

3. Make the ruffle

Decide how long you want the skirt and how long you want the ruffle. Subtract the ruffle length from the total skirt length and adjust the skirt pattern pieces by shortening or lengthening them, measuring up or down evenly from the original hemlines. Add SA. Make the ruffle pattern piece as described in the sidebar on page 45.

4. Label your pattern pieces

Label your pattern pieces with CF and/or CB, grain line, your style name, the name of each pattern piece (front and back skirt, front and back yoke, and ruffle), size or key measurements, and cutting instructions (front and back skirt pieces are "cut 1 on fold," yoke pieces are "cut 2 on fold," and ruffle is "cut 1").

Sewing instructions: Sew the skirt pieces together along the right-side seam only, and finish the raw edges. One set of yoke front and back pieces will be the facings; sew the outer yokes together along the right-side seam, and repeat for the facings. Press these seams open, and don't worry about finishing them, as they'll be enclosed. Now align the entire outer yoke to the yoke seam of the skirt, and stitch them together. Press both SAs toward the yoke.

With right sides together, seam the yoke facings to the outer yokes along the waist line. Press this seam open. Flip the facing to the inside and press the lower edge SA (½") under. Pin along the yoke seam line, and baste close to the folded edge. Then **edgestitch** the yoke seam and waistline from the outside of the skirt, and remove the basting. Now you can insert an **invisible zipper** along the left-side seam, and close up the lower seam, finishing the raw edges. Lastly, seam the short ends of your ruffle into one continuous loop, and run two rows of **gathering** stitches along the top edge. Gather it evenly to fit, and sew it to the bottom of the skirt. Finish this seam with an **overedge zigzag.** Hem the bottom edge of the ruffle, and go churn some butter!

p. 11

Skirt Variation 2: ROSIE SKIRT

This one's a sturdy little workwear-inspired number with a Center Front seam, a waistband, big patch pockets, and some sassy little side slits at the hem. You can use heavy-contrast topstitching thread to emphasize the utilitarian look. Herringbone denim, canvas, corduroy or heavy twill will all suit this style well. To begin, you'll need two pieces of paper, each a little longer than the desired length of your skirt, and smaller pieces for the waistband, pocket, and underlap.

1. ADD THE CF SEAM

Establish a clean edge or line at the left side of your paper, and draw a parallel line ½" to the right of it. Align your front skirt pattern from page 42 so that CF is on this line, and trace it onto the paper.

2. SHORTEN THE SKIRT

Measure up evenly from the original hem line to your desired skirt length (being sure to include 1" of SA). Notch the side seam 3" (2" + 1" SA) from the bottom to indicate the slits.

Repeat steps 1 and 2 for your back skirt pattern.

3. MAKE THE WAISTBAND

Depending on how low your skirt sits, and how curvy your hips are, there are two possible ways to make the waistband.

Method 1: If your hips are fairly straight (not significantly different from the waist of your skirt), or if your skirt sits high (near your true waist), you can use the straight waistband method, as described in the sidebar on page 45.

Method 2: If you are curvier, or if your skirt sits low on your hips, you'll need a shaped waistband. Along the waist line of your skirt pattern, measure down 1" to make a parallel curved line. Cut on this line. Do the same with your back skirt, so that you have trimmed 1" off the

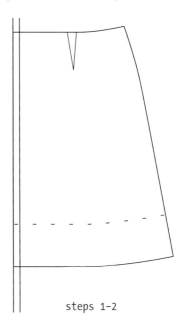

steps 1-2

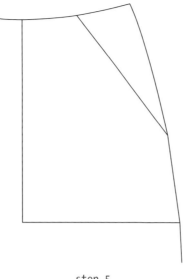

step 5

top of each skirt piece. Trim off the ½" of SA that was added at CF and CB on these waistband pieces. Label CF and CB on them so you don't get mixed up, and fold and tape the darts closed. Get a folded piece of paper and lay your front waistband piece so that CF is on the fold. Trace the piece onto the folded paper, and set the original aside. Now you can smooth out any bumps created when you folded the darts, and add SA to the top and bottom edge. Repeat with the back waistband piece. On the back piece, we also need to add a button extension to one side, so extend the waistband out by an additional inch. Cut out both waistband pieces with the paper folded. On the back piece, cut off the 1" extension on one side only, so the pattern piece is not symmetrical. Notch CF/CB on the waist seam of each piece and the side seam on the extension of the back waistband. Add SA by taping on paper to the waist line of the front and back skirt pieces, where the waistbands were cut off. Notch all four darts.

4. Make the underlap

In order to close this skirt with buttons, we'll need an underlap extension. On a small scrap of paper, make a rectangle that measures 3" wide (1" doubled + ½" SA + ½" SA) by the length you'd like your extension (4–5" should do it) + ½" SA + ½" SA.

5. Make the patch pocket

On a scrap of paper a bit bigger than you want your pocket to be, trace the upper portion of your front skirt pattern, with the dart taped shut. Using the waist line and side seam as two of the sides, draft a rectangular pocket to your liking, and draw a diagonal line across the upper corner, toward the side seam, to be the pocket opening. Remember to make it big enough for your hand to slip inside! Add ½" SA to the opening, left, and bottom edges of the pocket piece; the top and right sides already have it. Cut the pocket opening edge first, then fold it into a ¼" double-turned hem before cutting the rest of the sides. This will create extensions in the SA to allow for the hem.

6. Label your pattern pieces

Label your pattern pieces with CF and/or CB, grain line, your style name, the name of each pattern piece (front and back skirt, front and back waistband, underlap, and pocket), size or key measurements, and cutting instructions (front and back skirt pieces are "cut 2," front and back waistband are "cut 2," underlap is "cut 1," and pocket is "cut 2").

Sewing instructions: Sew all four darts. Stitch the CF and CB seams, using **flat-felled seams**. Hem the pocket opening edges with a double-turned ¼" hem, and press the center and bottom edges under by ½". Lay the pockets on your front skirt piece, aligning the top and side seam edges, and pin. Edgestitch the two pressed-under edges, and baste the top and side seam edges. Fold the underlap extension in half lengthwise, right sides facing, and stitch the two short edges. Turn right-side out and press. Place the underlap on the upper left-side seam of the back skirt, right sides together, aligning raw edges, and stitch. Now stitch the front skirt to the back along the side seams, from waist to notches on the right side, and from the bottom of the underlap to notches on the left side. Press these seams open, and finish with an overedge zigzag. Sew the front outer waistband to the back along the right-side seam, and press the seam open. Repeat for the waistband facings. Sew the outer waistband to the skirt along the waist line, making sure the back waistband extension matches up to the underlap. Sew the waistband facing, right sides facing, to the waistband, along the top edge and the two short edges. Flip the facing to the inside, tuck the lower edge under, and press. Baste the waistband seam from the inside, then edgestitch from the outside and remove the basting. Hem the skirt using a double-turned ½" hem, and **topstitch** around each side slit. Complete by making buttonholes in the front left waistband and along the front left-side seam, and stitching buttons to the back waistband and underlap, and you've got yourself a skirt!

The Fits-You-to-a-T-Shirt

Can you even imagine life without T-shirts? What would we wear? They've pretty much become default attire for anyone who gets to choose what they wear every day. If the occasion doesn't require you to wear some type of uniform, you probably reach for a T. Women, men, kids . . . even my dog wears them. And I'm not just talking about your standard-issue crew neck, short-sleeved model. Those have their place, but I'm referring to the general category of cut-and-sew knit shirts. They can be casual or dressy, simple or elaborate. Chances are, you're wearing one right now! I attribute the success of this ubiquitous style to two key factors: comfort and fit. Knit fabrics are constructed in a way that allows them to stretch. This means that a garment made of knit fabric will behave just as your skin does, expanding and shrinking as you move around.

So T-shirts feel very comfortable,

almost as if we're not wearing anything at all. This same quality, the innate stretchiness of knits, is also what makes knit garments fit a wide range of bodies. You can even wear a top that is smaller than you are, at least until you put it on. If you don't believe me, pull out one of your ribbed tank tops and measure across the chest while it's lying flat on a table. Double that number to get the full circumference, and then compare that to your chest size. Most of my tanks have a chest measurement of something like 24", but my chest measures 34" around, yet they fit me. See?

This brings up a key issue to consider when making a pattern, or when designing clothes in general: choice of fabric. The fabric you choose to construct your garment can absolutely determine whether it is a success or a failure. How many times have you seen the judges on *Project Runway* tell a designer that her choice of fabric ruined her chance of winning? It is one of the most common pitfalls, and something that can really only be learned through trial and error. The pattern and the fabric must work together. Patterns are drafted with a specific type of fabric–how it drapes, stretches, clings, or poofs–in mind. For example, if you take a pattern for a tight, fitted T-shirt that pulls on over the head, and stitch it up in a heavy cotton canvas, you won't even be able to put it on. And you wouldn't want to make a pair of cargo pants, with lots of pockets, flaps, and hardware, out of a sheer **tissue jersey.** These are extreme examples to illustrate a point, but the more subtle distinctions between, say, poplin, lawn, or voile, or even between the three possible **grain** options in any one fabric, can be much harder to perceive. But let's not get ahead of ourselves just yet. We're starting from the beginning, right?

The first, and most critical, characteristic of a fabric is how it is constructed. The two broad categories that nearly every fabric falls into are **woven** and **knit.** Understanding the difference between these two constructions, and how they behave, will give you a good foundation for getting to know the myriad options you have in the world of fabrics. And before you begin to make a new pattern, you must know which type you will be using.

Woven fabrics are constructed with two sets of yarns on the loom: the **warp** and the **weft.** The warp yarns, which run the length of the weave, are usually heavier and stronger. The weft yarns, which run back and forth across, alternating over and under each individual warp yarn, are generally lighter and not as strong. If you ever made woven potholders as a kid, you may remember that first you laid one set of yarns across the loom; this was the warp. Then you wove a second set, perpendicular to the first, by pulling them over, then under, each warp; this was your weft. This method of construction makes a very stable and sturdy, sometimes even rigid, cloth. Most pant or "bottom-weight" fabrics are wovens, such as denim, twill, corduroy, gabardine, canvas, and velvet. But many lightweight and sheer fabrics are woven as well, like poplin, voile, gauze, and crepe. Wovens, as a rule, have very little or no stretch. However, the addition of **spandex** to many woven fabrics in recent years has led to the development of a new category called **stretch wovens.** These are used mostly for pants, as the slight stretch improves fit and minimizes the bagginess that occurs after repeated wearings. Woven fabrics have three possible grain options: straight (also called lengthwise) grain, cross grain, and bias. **Straight grain** is the most common, with the heavier warp threads running vertically and giving

the garment good body, with a degree of **drape** in the horizontal direction. Cross grain, where the heavier warp threads run horizontally, gives a stiffer effect. If you want an extra-poufy bubble skirt that seems to defy gravity, cut it on the cross grain. Bias, which is the 45° angle exactly halfway between straight and cross grains, gives a very drapey, clingy effect with a hint of stretch.

Knit fabrics are constructed from one continuous yarn, running back and forth (or round and round in a tube) horizontally, each row looping and interlocking with the previous row. If you know how to knit by hand, the method will be completely familiar to you, though it can be hard to relate a chunky, three-stitches-per-inch gauge hand-knit scarf to a fine, sheer tissue jersey T-shirt, which may have up to 48 stitches per inch!

I've never seen it comprise more than 10 percent of the fiber content of any fabric, whether it's a woven or a knit. Knits are usually cut on the straight grain, so that the stretch is horizontal.

Now that you have at least a basic understanding of the two types of fabric, I can explain why you'll need to decide which type you're going to use before you even begin your pattern. This involves another major principle of patternmaking: ease.

There are actually two different kinds of ease in the world of sewing. One is when you seam together two pieces of fabric, one of which is slightly larger than the other, to add a hint of shaping. The other is the one I'm talking about here; it is the difference

The fabric you choose to construct your garment can absolutely determine whether it is a success or a failure.

Jersey, the most common knit fabric, is the exact same stitch as stockinette in hand knitting. Cool, right? This looping construction gives knit fabrics a much more fluid, stretchy, drapey quality than wovens. They can be trickier to sew, but their flexibility makes it worthwhile to learn how to handle them. All kinds of T-shirt fabrics—jersey, rib, interlock, thermal—are knits, as are fleece, French terry, pointelle, and velour. Adding spandex to knits makes them incredibly stretchy, and even more importantly, gives them good **recovery**. Recovery means that the fabric will bounce back to its original state again and again, as opposed to stretching out and staying there. Bathing suits, leggings, and dancewear are nearly always made using knits with spandex. Note, though, that spandex is never used for a fabric by itself; it's more like an additive.

between the actual body measurements and the pattern measurements. Another way to think about it is the amount of space between the wearer and the garment. In most woven garments, even when you want them to fit very closely, you will want to add at least 1–2" of ease to the pattern to allow a little breathing room. Because wovens don't stretch, we also need to allow extra space to accommodate movement of the body. For example, if I wrap a tape measure around my arm just above the elbow, it measures just under 10". But when I bend my elbow to its full extent, my arm expands to 11". You have probably also noticed that your sleeves get a bit shorter when you bend your elbows. And of course you want your coat to fit over a chunky sweater. These are the kinds of reasons why we add a dash, or a dollop, of extra room in our patterns, which I call **functional ease.**

The other reason to add ease is much more subjective. Peasant blouses, parachute pants, and belted tunics are examples of styles that are meant to "fit" in an oversized way. Your own personal taste or ideas, combined with the styling trends of the decade or moment, will affect whether you make a piece that fits closely to the body, or something that hangs freely from the shoulders or hips, bearing little resemblance to the actual shape or size of the person underneath it. This I call **stylistic ease**.

As I mentioned before, in the example with the ribbed tank top, there are times when the pattern measurements may even be smaller than the body measurements. This is known as **negative ease**. Negative ease can only be used for patterns that will be constructed in the stretchiest knits, like **rib** or spandex knits, and never for wovens.

We've established that the T-shirt pattern we are about to begin will be made in a knit. It's best to get even a little more specific than this, as there are a wide range of knit fabrics with varying characteristics, so for our purposes let's call it a standard cotton jersey. This tells us that there will be some stretch, but not a huge amount.

BASIC T

A basic T-shirt pattern (that fits you exactly as you like) will be a key component of your library. You can use it to make yourself long- and short-sleeved tops, tanks, sweatshirts, tunics, dresses . . . but I'm getting ahead of myself. Let's keep it simple to begin. We'll make this shirt to fit close to the body, and you can test it out in a variety of knits, like jersey, rib, interlock, thermal, pointelle; in different fibers; with and without spandex. You'll find you might need to adjust the pattern for certain knits to make it snugger or looser, depending on the stretchiness of the knit.

MEASUREMENTS

Bust circumference* (at fullest point)

Waist circumference* (at smallest point)

Distance from high shoulder point down to waist

Hip circumference* (where you want the bottom of the shirt to be)

Length of shirt (high shoulder point to hem)

Shoulder width**

Neck width**

Front neck drop

Sleeve length

Bicep circumference**

Wrist circumference**

*For each of these horizontal measurements, divide by four. These quarter measurements will be the ones you use for drafting the pattern. They will be referred to as quarter-bust, quarter-waist, and quarter-hip.

**Divide these measurements by two. These will be referred to as half-shoulder, half-neck, etc.

MAKE THE FRONT SHIRT

1. PREPARE YOUR PAPER

Begin with a piece of paper approximately 4" longer than the length of your shirt, and at least 2" wider than your quarter-bust or -hip, whichever is bigger. Make sure at least one of the long sides of the paper is a perfectly straight, smooth edge. If it isn't, draw a line with your ruler close to the edge, and cut on the line. All of your drafting will begin from this edge, so it's important that it is straight and clean. Orient your paper so that this edge is on the left side. This edge will become Center Front (CF) on your shirt.

2. PLOT THE LENGTH

Along your straight left-side edge (a.k.a. CF), make a small cross-mark about 2" down from the top edge of the paper. From this point, measure down the length of your shirt (high shoulder point to hem) and make another mark there.

3. PLOT THE SHOULDER

At the top mark, align your clear ruler so that it intersects CF at a 90° angle (a.k.a. perpendicular). Draw a horizontal line here that measures your half-shoulder. This is your shoulder line. Make sure the endpoint of the line is clear; make a cross-mark or dot to define it.

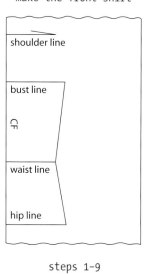

make the front shirt

shoulder line

bust line

CF

waist line

hip line

steps 1–9

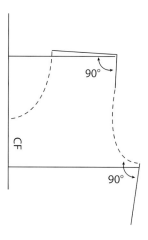

90°

CF

90°

steps 10–11

4. Plot the hip

Draw another horizontal line at the mark you made at the bottom of the paper, using your quarter-hip measurement. This will be your hip line, which in this context is the bottom edge of your shirt.

5. Plot the waist

From the shoulder line, along CF, measure down the distance from your high shoulder point to your waist. Make a mark, and from this point draft a line perpendicular to CF, which measures your quarter-waist.

6. Plot the bust line

To determine the proper placement for the bust, we must first decide the size of our armhole. Take a look down at your armpits, and you'll see that they basically are right on the same horizontal line as your bust. So the bottom of the armhole will be the very same point as the top of the side seam, or in other words, the bust line. Now, figure out what size your armhole should be (see sidebar above). Measure down that amount from the shoulder line, and make a mark. From this point you can plot out your quarter-bust measurement.

7. Plot the neck points

On the shoulder line, measuring from CF, mark your half-neck width. On CF, measuring down from the shoulder line, mark your front neck drop.

8. Add shoulder slope

Because our shoulders have a slight angle to them, we'll give our pattern a bit of **shoulder slope**. At the point where you marked your neck width, measure up ¼" and make a mark. Connect this point to your shoulder point. This new line is now your shoulder seam line, and replaces the old horizontal one. Cross out or erase the old one so you don't get confused later.

9. Connect the dots

Now we can begin connecting the dots so we'll have a semblance of your pattern. Leaving the neck and armhole spaces empty for now, draw a line from the bust/underarm point to the waist point, and from there to the hip point. Aha! It's like seeing a bunch of random stars become the Big Dipper, only this constellation is a map of your body!

10. Plot the armhole

All we have left are the bendy bits—the armhole curve and the neckline. To begin the

armhole, let's establish two 90° angles right off the bat. Hold your ruler perpendicular to the shoulder seam line, at the outer end or shoulder point. Draw a line about 2" downward from that point. Now hold the ruler perpendicular to the side seam line, at the underarm point, and draw a line about ½" long, toward the CF. These two short lines are the foundation of your armhole. The curve you draw *must* begin and end on these lines, so that the corners will be 90° angles. Using the roundest part of your hip curve, see if you can find a spot where it meets up with both lines, so they are connected into one smooth, continuous curved line. The top two-thirds of your armhole will be fairly straight, starting out as the 2" straight line that runs perpendicular from the shoulder point, curving slightly to the right in the middle, and then sharply bending toward the right to meet the ½" line that is perpendicular to the side seam.

11. Plot the neckline

At the high shoulder point, hold your ruler perpendicular to the shoulder line, and draw a ½" line. Draw another line at your front neck drop point, from CF. Now, either use your hip curve or French curve, or just draw freehand, a nice smoothly curved neckline,

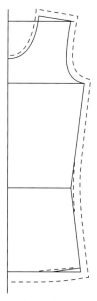

steps 12–14

Determining Your Armhole Measurement

When measuring the armhole of a garment, we usually just measure a straight line (even though the actual armhole is a curve) from the point where the **shoulder seam** intersects the sleeve, down to the point where the **underarm seam** meets the side seam. A standard armhole measurement for a medium-sized fitted T-shirt is about 7" to 7½". To figure out what will be best for you, grab some favorite tops from your closet and measure the armholes. If they tend toward 6½–7", go with 6¾", and likewise if they're bigger. Or if you know your shirts always feel as if they're pinching at the pits, or conversely if you usually feel as if you're swimming in them, add or subtract an inch accordingly. You'll fine-tune this once you make a muslin and try it on, so for now just take your best guess.

connecting the two ½" lines. It should approximate a quarter-circle or quarter-oval, depending on the measurements you chose for your neck width and drop.

12. SQUARE THE CORNERS

Just like with the skirt, we need to make any remaining un-squared corners into right angles. If you've done everything correctly thus far, the only one should be at the bottom where the side seam meets the hem. Hold your ruler perpendicular to the side seam, and slide it up and down until the ruler intersects the hem line two-thirds of the way over from CF (closer to side seam). Draw a line, and erase or cross out the old one.

13. SMOOTH THE POINTS

Now we need to smooth out those obtuse angles and make them into curves. There's one at your waist point and the one you just made in the previous step. Take your curve tool, and lay it down alongside one of those angles. Slide the curve around until you find a section of it that fits nicely into the angle. The edge of the hip curve should be *touching* your line at points a few inches to each side of the angle. Following the curve, draw a line between the two points. Erase or mark out the old line. Repeat for the other angle.

14. ADD SEAM ALLOWANCE

The last step is to add your ½" (or ⅝") SA. On curves, hold the ruler perpendicular to your seam line, and make a dot ½" out from the seam line. Now slide the ruler over a bit and repeat. Just be sure the ruler is always held exactly 90° to the seam. The curvier the section of line, the closer together your dots should be. Then connect those dots. On straighter sections, add the SA by holding the ruler parallel to the seam line and ½" over it. Keep shifting the ruler to continue the SA along slight curves. Perfectly straight lines can be dealt with in one pass.

Tip: I like to add a full inch of SA along the bottom hip line, so I can do a ½" double-turned hem. Think about how you plan to hem your T-shirt, and add your SA accordingly. Hemming knits can be tricky, and most of them don't unravel, so I often leave the edges completely raw. However, jersey knits always roll, so a little seam allowance compensates for the length lost in rolling.

Another part of the pattern where a different size of SA is generally used is the neckline. Because it is such a small curved area, we usually use only a ¼" SA to minimize distortion.

15. CHECK YOUR WORK

Your first piece of the T-shirt pattern is now finished, but before you cut it out, let's just do a quick once-over.

* *Did you double-check that all six corners (CF neck, high shoulder point, shoulder point, top of side seam, bottom of side seam, CF hip) are right angles?*

* *Did you check that there aren't any other pointy bits aside from those six corners?* They should have been smoothed out into curves, just before adding the SA.

* *Does the basic size and shape of the shirt look right to you?* It should look pretty recognizable at this point as half of a shirt that would fit you, so if anything looks really wacky, go back and check your measurements, and go over the steps again.

Curves Ahead: Navigating Those Nebulous Curves

Many of the pattern lines we draft practically draw themselves; we plot certain points and then simply connect the dots. The shoulder, side seam, and hip (hem) lines in this pattern are all that way: no-brainers. But some of the lines, or rather curves, like the armhole and neckline, require a little more, uh, *je ne sais quoi*. Once you are a little more experienced, you can pretty much draw these freehand. But at the beginning level, your eyeballs haven't yet ogled many of these curves in pattern form. Part of the problem is that we're trying to translate three-dimensional, multiplaned curves into a flat, two-dimensional pencil line on a piece of paper. Even worse, in a pattern, you're looking at only a quarter (for the neck) or half (for the armhole) of the full curve.

A nice, easy exercise to illustrate what I'm talking about is this: Take a piece of paper (a small square or rectangle will do fine) and fold it in half, then in half again. Draw a quarter-circle from one of the folded sides to the other. Cut on the curved line you drew. Unfold the paper and assess the shape: If it's a true circle, you're a natural. But more likely it's sort of square-ish, or pointy, or like a four-leaf clover. You also might see why the 90° angles are so important now, because if either end of your quarter-circle line intersected the fold in anything other than a right angle, it will have made a point when you opened it up. Don't worry; these principles will become clearer as you gain experience. Every time you draft a curve on paper and then see how it behaves once it becomes a muslin on the body, you will learn a bit more about how this all works.

make the sleeve

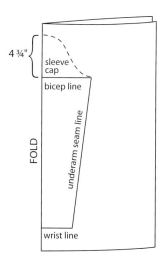

steps 1–3

16. Cut it out

To save time, tape, pin, or staple the second piece of paper behind the one you made the front pattern on. This will become your back piece. Then go ahead and cut through both layers, starting at the bottom. When you reach the top, cut the shoulder, then continue straight across to CF, leaving the neckline uncut. Separate the two pieces and continue to cut out the neckline on the front piece. The remaining piece will become the back.

Make the Back Shirt

1. Transfer some reference points

To begin the back pattern, lay the new back piece that you cut out in step 16 of the front shirt on top of the front pattern. Trace the shoulder seam line and the front neckline onto the back pattern. The straight edge of the paper on the left is now Center Back (CB). Remove the front and set it aside. Now you can draw a back neckline, using the front neckline as reference. Back neck drops are usually pretty small—anywhere from ½" to 1". But your front neckline will help you determine where the back should be; for example,

a summery tank top with a wide and deep front neckline might have a back neck drop of 3" or 4". Draw something that looks right to you, making sure it hits CB at a 90° angle, of course, and that it meets the shoulder seam (also at a right angle) at the exact same point as the front neckline.

2. Add seam allowance and cut

Add ¼" SA to your new back neckline. All that's left to cut is the back neck, and you're finished with this piece. Hooray!

Make the Sleeve

1. Prepare your paper

Wrangle yourself a piece of paper that is 4" longer than your sleeve length measurement and 4" wider than your full bicep circumference. Fold the paper in half lengthwise, and keep it folded with the folded edge on your left. We'll be drafting half of the sleeve and then unfolding the paper, so that we have a whole sleeve pattern. We do this because we'll want to cut out two sleeves from the fabric, as opposed to just one front and back piece cut on the fold.

2. Plot the length and wrist

Along the fold, make a mark about 2" down from the top of your paper. From this point, measure down the length of your sleeve, and make another mark. From here, hold your ruler perpendicular to the fold and draw a line that measures your half-wrist circumference.

3. Make the cap

The **sleeve cap** is the curve at the top of your sleeve, which is shaped like a bell. Before we can draft the cap, we'll need to determine our cap height. I use a formula of two-thirds (.67) times armhole height (see Determining Your Armhole Measurement, page 61). So if you used an armhole height of 7", your cap height will be 4¾" (I rounded to the nearest ¼"). Measure down 4¾" from the top mark on your paper. From this point, draw a line, perpendicular to the fold, that measures your half-bicep circumference. Connect this bicep point with your wrist point; this is the underarm seam line. OK, now we're ready to draft that bell-shaped cap! Start by establishing a 90° angle (from the fold) at the top point of your sleeve; just draw a short ½" line or so.

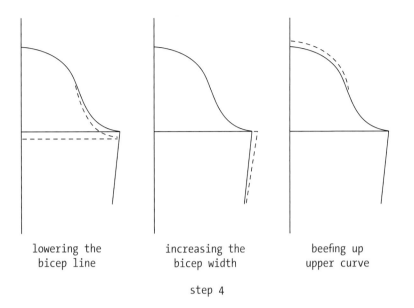

lowering the
bicep line

increasing the
bicep width

beefing up
upper curve

step 4

1/3

step 5

Then hold the ruler perpendicular to the underarm seam line, and draw another ½" line, toward the fold. Now connect these two short lines by curving downward from the top one, and curving upward from the lower one, meeting in a very smooth S-curve. Make sure that where the two opposing curves meet, the transition is seamless (see diagram). It should almost be a straight line for about an inch or two.

4. Check the sleeve cap

The seam line you just created for your sleeve cap will be sewn to the armhole of your T-shirt, so we must make sure the two lines fit together. On your sleeve pattern, measure the exact length of your sleeve cap seam line, and on your front shirt pattern, measure the length along your armhole curve (not the straight armhole height), excluding SA. Compare the two measurements. If they are equal, or if the sleeve cap seam is up to ½" bigger than the armhole, you're in good shape. But if the sleeve cap is *smaller* than the armhole, you'll have to adjust it until they are at least equal. You can increase the cap seam length by lowering your bicep line, increasing your bicep width, or beef-

ing up the upper part of the curve (see diagram). None of these adjustments should be too drastic, that is, not more than ¼" from the original line. You might need to do a combination of two or three of these methods. Play around with the cap seam line until the two measurements match or the sleeve cap is slightly bigger (this bit of ease will give the cap some shaping to cup your shoulder).

5. Square the wrist corner

We're on the home stretch! Down at the wrist point, extend the underarm seam line by about 1", then hold your ruler perpendicular to it. Slide the ruler up and down until it intersects the wrist line about one-third of the way over from the underarm seam to the fold. Draw a line from the extended underarm seam line to the wrist line.

6. Smooth the wrist line

Using your curve tool, blend the obtuse angle you just made in the wrist line so that it is a nice smooth curve. Be careful not to alter either of the two right angles at each end of the wrist.

7. Add seam allowance

Add ½" (or ⅝") SA to the cap curve and the underarm seam. Add 1" (or your preference) to the wrist.

8. Cut it out

With the paper still folded, cut out the sleeve, being careful not to let the underside slide around while you're cutting.

Make the Neckband

1. Determine measurements

On your front and back pattern pieces, using your tape measure, measure the circumference of your neck opening. Be sure to measure both the front and back necklines, on the seam line (not the seam allowance line), excluding the seam allowance at the shoulder seam. Add the front to the back, and double this total to get the full circumference. For mine, the front neckline measured 7" and the back was 4", so together they equal 11", and doubling that gives me 22" for my full neckline circumference. Next, because the neckband needs to be slightly smaller than the neck seam to lie flat, subtract 10% of that total.

True Love

Every time you make a pattern, the last thing you'll do after cutting it out is *true* it. You wouldn't want to waste time making a muslin before checking that there are no obvious errors, would you? Of course not. So take each pattern piece, one at a time, and lay it on top of the piece it will be seamed to, along the seam line. If the seam is straight, or if both pieces have the same shape along the seam line you're checking, it's simple to see if they match. But if the shapes are different, you will need to "walk" one seam line against the other. Take one piece and put a pushpin through one end of the seam. Then lay it over its partner piece, and poke the pushpin through the beginning of the same seam on that piece, so the pin is through both patterns and they are aligned at the same point. Determine how much of the two seam lines are lying exactly on top of each other, and move the pushpin to the point where they begin to diverge. Rotate, or "walk" the top pattern, to align the next section of seam, and move the pushpin again. Continue to do this until you reach the other end of the seam lines to confirm that they match. If not, adjust one or both patterns until they do. **Note:** All trueing must be done using the seam lines, not seam allowance lines. These can be very different, especially along curves.

This is your neckband length. Subtracting 10% (or about 2¼") gave me 19¾" for my neckband length.

2. Draft the pattern

Now we can draft the pattern for the neckband, which will be a simple rectangle. Begin by drawing a line on your paper the length of your neckband, plus 1" for SA (that's ½" on each end). We are going to make the finished band ½" wide, so to determine the width of the pattern, double the finished width (that gives us 1") and add ¼" SA for each side (that's another ½"). Thus our total width will be 1½". Measure 1½" up from your first line and draw a parallel line. Fill in the two short ends and you've got your pattern. Fold it in half so the short ends meet. Draw a line on the fold; this is your grain line.

3. True your pattern

The final checking-over of pattern pieces is called trueing the pattern. This is when you check that all corners that will be intersecting seams or edges are squared, and that the overall shape and size generally look right. Most importantly, you should check that all seam lines are exactly the same length as the corresponding seam line on the piece it will be seamed to. Thus far, we have been making our back pattern pieces by tracing our fronts, so it's pretty much a guarantee that the front and back seams will fit together. And we've checked that our sleeve cap fits our armhole. Going forward, as our patterns become more complex, it will become more important to check that the two sides of every seam match. Their shapes may be different (as with the sleeve cap and armhole), but the lengths must be the same, unless you plan to gather or ease one into the other (see How Much to Spread? on page 128).

4. Label your pattern pieces

Label your pattern pieces with CF and/or CB, grain line, your style name, the name of each pattern piece (front, back, neckband, and sleeve), size or key measurements, and cutting instructions (front and back pieces are "cut 1 on fold," neckband is "cut 1," and the sleeves are "cut 2"). Notch the top of the sleeve cap on the fold.

Sewing instructions: Remember that when sewing knits, you'll need to use either a **stretch stitch** or a tiny zigzag (I find 1.5–2mm for length and width works well). Sew front to back at the shoulder and side seams. Sew the short ends of the neckband together, and fold the band lengthwise, with wrong sides facing. Pin the band to the right side of the neckline, aligning all raw edges, and stitch. (For a more detailed description, see the section on T-shirt neckbands in Insider Sewing Techniques, page 149.) Sew the underarm seam of sleeves and set sleeves into armholes. Hem the cuff and the bottom edges of the shirt with a double-turned ½" hem.

Tip: Shoulder seams of T-shirts have a tendency to stretch out and creep down your arms. You may wish to insert a nonstretchable trim into your shoulder seams to prevent them from stretching out. Twill tape, seam binding, or a thin ribbon work well. Just pin the trim in as you pin the seam together, and stitch through all three layers at once.

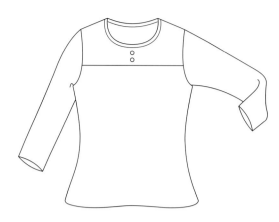

T-Shirt Variation 1: MARGUERITE T

You can use your Basic T pattern from page 58 to create endless variations! Adding a simple interior seam is an easy way to add some interest and play with color blocking or pattern mixing. In this project we'll add a classic yoke seam and some trims for a fun, French-inspired take on your Basic T. I used solid and printed cotton/rayon jerseys; you could also try ribs or pointelle knits. You'll need one or two pieces of paper (one if you only want a front yoke; two if you want a back yoke as well), slightly bigger than your front and back Basic T patterns.

1. MAKE THE YOKE SEAM

Trace a copy of your front pattern piece from your Basic T on page 60. With your ruler, decide where you would like to place the yoke seam; somewhere between the neck drop and the bottom of the armhole, and not less than 1" from either. If this isn't possible, you'll need to raise your neck drop and adjust the neckline accordingly (just follow the instructions for the Basic T neckline, using a higher neck drop) before drawing your yoke. Draw the line perpendicular to CF. Cut on the line and tape a scrap of paper to each of these cut edges. Add SA to each side of your yoke seams, and cut the excess paper away.

Repeat for the back pattern if you want to have a yoke in the back as well. Could that have been any easier? Isn't this fun?

2. LABEL AND TRUE YOUR PATTERN PIECES

Label your pattern pieces with CF and/or CB, grain line, your style name, the name of each pattern piece (front and back yoke, front and back bodice, and sleeve), size or key measurements, and cutting instructions (yoke and bodice pieces are "cut 1 on fold"; sleeves are "cut 2"). Check that all corresponding pieces match along seam lines.

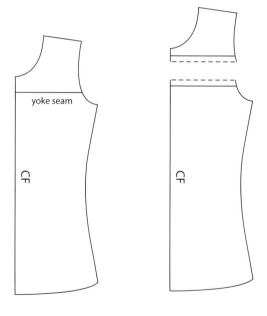

step 1

Note: For this style, you'll use the same sleeve as the original T-shirt sleeve, so it's up to you if you want to make a copy of it to keep with this pattern or just make a note on the front to use your "Basic T Sleeve" pattern. I shortened mine to ¾-length, but you could leave them long.

SEWING INSTRUCTIONS: To get the most impact from a yoke, cut it from a **contrast** fabric. Try different colors, prints with solids, or contrasting fabrics and textures, such as a woven yoke on a knit T. It's up to you if the sleeve matches the body or the yoke. Play with your options! I just wouldn't recommend cutting the sleeve out of a woven, as the pattern was made to be a knit and would most likely be too tight. Start sewing with the yoke seam(s), right sides together, using a stretch or small zigzag stitch. Topstitch or edgestitch if desired. From here on out it's just your basic T-shirt construction; refer to the sewing instructions on page 58. Try finishing the neckline with a stretchy trim and a couple of tiny buttons at CF, and call it a day!

p. 13

T-Shirt Variation 2: CHARLOTTE TOP

With this one, you'll start to see how a few simple effects can increase your style options exponentially! We'll begin by making a little drawstring casing at the neckline, in which you can insert a sweet silk ribbon, a crochet chain, a shoelace, or even a string that's simply a cut strip of jersey (its natural tendency to roll makes it a cord with no sewing necessary). It's all about adding your own personality at this point. We'll also put an elastic casing on the shortened sleeves for a hint of **shirring**, transforming the plain-Jane T into the romantic Charlotte Top. You'll want a lightweight, soft knit for this one because of the gathered neckline and sleeves; I used a nice heathered tissue jersey. You'll need three pieces of paper: two a little bigger than your front and back Basic T patterns from page 58, and one a few inches wider than your Basic T sleeve pattern.

1. SCOOP OUT YOUR NECKLINE

For this style you'll want a neckline that is somewhat lower and wider than your original T-shirt neckline (page 58). Trace a copy of both your front and back Basic T pattern pieces from page 58. Don't line up the CF and CB edges with the edge of the paper; leave at least an inch of space there. Don't cut the copies out yet. On the front, lower the neck drop to around 7", and increase the neck width to around 9". (Remember, though, that since this is a horizontal measurement, you'll only use half for the pattern piece, so that's 4½".) Draw a new neckline, just as you did the first time, using these measurements. Do the same on the back, with a new neck drop of around 3". Add SA (usually ¼" on necklines).

2. ADD FULLNESS TO THE FRONT AND BACK

Next we'll need to add a bit of fullness at CF and CB so that the drawstring will have something to gather. Starting with the front piece, in the space you left between CF and the edge of the paper, draw a line 1" to the left and parallel to CF. Extend the neck and hemlines to meet the new line. Repeat for the back pattern. Now you can cut out your new pattern pieces.

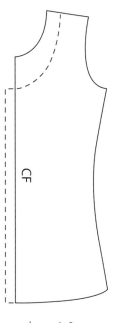

steps 1–2

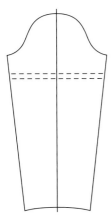

step 4

3. Make the drawstring casing neckband

With your tape measure, measure the circumference of your neck opening on your new front and back patterns. Measure both the front and back necklines, directly on the seam line (*not* the seam allowance line), excluding the SA at the shoulder seam. Add the front (mine was 10½") to the back (mine was 7¼"), and double this total (17¾" x 2 = 35½") to get the full circumference. The pattern for the casing will be a simple rectangle. Begin by drawing a line on your paper, the length of your neck measurement, plus 1" for SA (that's ½" on each end). We are going to make the finished casing ¾" wide, so to determine the width of the pattern, double the finished width (that gives us 1½") and add seam allowance for each side (if we're using ¼" SA, that's another ½"). Thus our total width will be 2". Measure 2" up from your first line, and draw a parallel line. Fill in the two short ends and you've got your pattern. Fold it in half so the short ends meet. Draw a line on the fold; this is your grain line and also CB.

Note: You could also make this pattern half the length you need and cut it on the fold. Just be sure to label this clearly!

4. Shorten the sleeve and add fullness

Trace a copy of your sleeve pattern from page 63. Measure down about 7" from the top of your sleeve cap (a little longer or shorter if you like, just so it's at least 1½" longer than your sleeve cap) and draw a line across, perpendicular to the center line of the sleeve. Now we need to add a bit more for the elastic casing. The casing will be ½" wide, so we'll add ½" to the bottom of the pattern. Now draw a vertical line down the center of your sleeve, from the top of the cap to the bottom edge. Starting from the bottom edge, cut along this line, stopping ¼" from the top so that the pieces are still connected. Spread the bottom apart by 2" and tape a new piece of paper behind it to fill in the gap. Smooth out the bottom edge into a slight curve. Lastly, add ½" SA to the bottom edge of your sleeve, and it's all done.

5. Label and true your pattern pieces

Label your pattern pieces with CF and/or CB, grain line, your style name, the name of each pattern piece (front, back, neckband casing, and sleeve), size or key measurements, and cutting instructions (front and back are "cut 1 on fold," the sleeves are "cut 2," the casing is

"cut 1"). Check that all corresponding pieces match along seam lines.

Sewing instructions: Sew front to back along side and shoulder seams. Hem two short edges of neckband by turning ¼" and then ¼" again and stitching. Fold neckband lengthwise, wrong sides together, and pin to right side of shirt neckline, matching all three raw edges, so that the short hemmed edges meet at CF. Stitch with a stretch stitch or small zigzag stitch. Turn the band in toward neck, and topstitch the seam, if desired. Measure a length of ¼" elastic so that it is snug (not tight!) against your bicep, and add 1". Cut 2 pieces of elastic this length. Join the ends of elastic together by overlapping 1" and stitching across, forming two rings. Sew the underarm seam of sleeve. Pin one elastic ring to the wrong side of the bottom edge of the sleeve, turn edge ½" and then ½" again (wrapping around elastic) and stitch, being careful not to catch the elastic in your stitches. Attach the sleeves to shirt. Hem the shirt as desired, and lace your drawstring of choice through the neck casing.

The Button-Down Shirt

Let's talk for just a minute about a term I mentioned earlier: *functional ease*. Whereas a knit shirt can be exactly the same measurements as (or even smaller than) your body, woven shirts require a bit of breathing room. Because they don't stretch, woven fabrics can't move and bend with you the way knits do. So giving yourself a little space between your skin and the garment will allow you to reach, twist, laugh, and dance without fear of busting a stitch!

To incorporate functional ease into your shirt, you'll need to add something like 2-4" to all of your full body circumference measurements in advance.

By *full body circumference*, I mean the measurements that go all the way around your body, like bust, waist, and hip. Be consistent; if you decide to add 3", add it to all these measurements. Add half of your designated ease amount to the half-body measurements, like shoulder width and neck width, and the smaller full circumference measurements like bicep and wrist. Note that you'll only be adding ease to *horizontal* measurements, not vertical ones like length and neck drops.

How much ease should you add? Well, this is up to you. It's partly a matter of your size; a petite person would tend to need less than a tall, Rubenesque one. And it's largely a matter of taste and aesthetics. If you like your clothes to be fairly fitted, two inches of ease (distributed around the full circumference of the garment) might be plenty. But if you prefer a roomier, more oversized look, you might want four inches or even more. Experiment to see what works best for you.

BASIC SHIRT

There's nothing more classic than a woven collared shirt. Whether it's a menswear-style button-down, a Western cowboy-inspired number, or a girly, ruffly blouse, woven shirts are infinitely versatile and wearable. Feel like making one? You've got lots of options for fabric: Cotton shirtings, quilting prints, eyelet, voile, chambray, pinwale cord, really almost any light- to medium-weight woven will do! The measurements you'll need are the same ones you needed for the Basic T pattern on page 58, with the addition of functional ease (subsequently referred to as *FE*).

MEASUREMENTS

Bust circumference + FE* (at the fullest point)

Waist circumference + FE* (at smallest point)

Distance from HSP down to waist

Hip circumference + FE* (where you want the bottom of the shirt to be)

Length of shirt (HSP to hem)

Shoulder width + ¼" FE**

Neck width** (see Determining Your Front Neck Drop and Neck Width, page 78)

Front neck drop (see Determining Your Front Neck Drop and Neck Width, page 78)

Sleeve length

Bicep circumference + ¼" FE**

Wrist circumference + ¼" FE**

For each of these horizontal measurements, divide by four. These quarter measurements will be the ones you use for drafting the pattern. They will be referred to as quarter-bust, quarter-waist, *and* quarter-hip.

**Divide these measurements by two. These will be referred to as half-shoulder, half-neck, etc.*

MAKE THE FRONT SHIRT

1. PREPARE YOUR PAPER

Begin with a piece of paper, approximately 4" longer than the length of your shirt (HSP to hem), and at least 4" wider than your quarter-bust or -hip, whichever is bigger. Make sure at least one of the long sides of the paper is a perfectly straight, smooth edge. If it isn't, draw a line with your ruler close to the edge, and cut on the line. All your drafting will begin from this edge, so it's important that it is straight and clean. Orient your paper so that this edge is on the left side.

2. ESTABLISH CENTER FRONT (CF)

Whereas in the Basic T pattern (page 60) the left edge of the paper automatically became CF, this shirt will have a fold-back button placket, so you will need extra room in the pattern to fold back and form the placket. We are going to make a 1"-wide placket, so you'll need 2" extra beyond CF. Use this formula to determine how much you need for the placket: Placket width (1") + ½ placket width (½") + ½" SA = 2". So to make the placket and establish your CF line, draw a line, parallel to the left edge of your paper, 2" over from the edge. This line is CF, so you can begin drafting the rest of the pattern from here.

make the front shirt

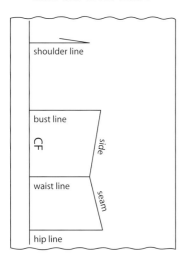

steps 1–10

3. PLOT THE LENGTH

Along CF, make a small cross-mark about 2" down from the top edge of the paper. From this point, measure down the length of your shirt (HSP to hem) and make another mark there.

4. PLOT THE SHOULDER

At the top mark, align your clear ruler so that it intersects CF at 90°. Draw a horizontal line here that measures your half-shoulder. This is your shoulder line. Make sure the endpoint of the line is clear; make a cross-mark or dot to define it.

5. PLOT THE HIP

Draw another horizontal line at the mark you made at the bottom of the paper, using your quarter-hip measurement. This will be your hip line, which in this context is the bottom edge of your shirt.

6. PLOT THE WAIST

From the shoulder line, along CF, measure down the distance from your high shoulder point to your waist. Make a mark, and from this point draft a line, perpendicular to CF, which measures your quarter-waist.

7. PLOT THE BUST LINE

To determine the proper placement for the bust, we must first decide the size of our armhole. The bottom of the armhole will be the very same point as the top of the side seam, or in other words, the bust line. Now, let's figure out what size your armhole should be. Find the measurement you used in your Basic T pattern (see Determining Your Armhole Measurement, page 61), and add 1–2", depending on your preference for fitted or roomier armholes. Measure down that amount from the shoulder line, and make a

---

Determining Your Front Neck Drop and Neck Width

So far, our only encounter with neck drops and widths has been in the Basic T pattern. In that case, the measurements were mostly a style decision, whether you wanted a high or low, wide, or narrow neckline for your top. However, for this woven shirt we will be making a collar, and your neck drop and width will determine the placement of the seam where the collar is attached to the shirt. Therefore, the drop should be a fairly

traditional placement, right at the base of your neck where your two clavicle bones meet. On me, that's at about $3^{1}/_{2}$" down from my high shoulder point (HSP). The width should be the distance between your two HSPs. On me, that's about 7". You can play around with more adventurous collars and seams when you've got a little more experience, but for now let's just keep it simple!

---

mark. From this point you can plot out your quarter-bust measurement.

8. PLOT THE NECK POINTS
On the shoulder line, measuring from CF, mark your half-neck width. On CF, measuring down from the shoulder line, mark your front neck drop.

9. ADD SHOULDER SLOPE
Because our shoulders have a slight angle to them, we'll give our pattern a bit of shoulder slope. At the point where you marked your neck width, measure up ¼" and make a mark. Connect this point to your shoulder point. This new line is now your shoulder seam line, and replaces the old horizontal one. Cross out or erase the old one so you don't get confused later.

10. CONNECT THE DOTS
Now we can begin connecting the dots, so we'll have a semblance of our pattern. Leaving the neck and armhole spaces empty for now, draw a line from the bust/underarm point to the waist point, and from there to the hip point. This will be the side seam. Your shirt is starting to take shape!

11. PLOT THE ARMHOLE
You should remember how we created the armhole and neckline curves for the T-shirt pattern. To begin the armhole, establish two 90° angles right off the bat. Hold your ruler perpendicular to the shoulder seam line, at the outer end or shoulder point. Draw a line about 2" downward from that point. Now hold the ruler perpendicular to the side seam line, at the underarm point, and draw a line about ½" long, toward CF. These two short lines are the foundation of your armhole. The curve you draw *must* begin and end on these lines, so that the corners will be 90°. Using the roundest part of your hip curve, see if you can find a spot where it meets up with both

lines, so that they are connected into one smooth, continuous curved line. The top two-thirds of your armhole will be fairly straight, starting out as the 2" straight line that runs perpendicular from the shoulder point, curving very slightly to the right in the middle, and then sharply bending toward the right to meet the ½" line that is perpendicular to the side seam.

12. PLOT THE NECKLINE
At the high shoulder point, hold your ruler perpendicular to the shoulder line, and draw a ½" line. Do the same at your front neck drop point, from CF. Now, either use your hip curve or French curve, or just draw freehand, a nice smoothly curved neckline connecting the two ½" lines. It should approximate a quarter-circle or quarter-oval, depending on the measurements you chose for your neck width and drop.

13. SQUARE THE CORNERS
As always, we need to make any remaining un-squared corners into right angles. If you've done everything correctly thus far, the only one should be at the bottom, where the side seam meets the hem. Hold your ruler perpendicular to the side seam, and slide it up and down until the ruler intersects the hemline two-thirds of the way over from CF (closer to the side seam). Draw a line, and erase or cross out the old one.

14. SMOOTH THE POINTS
All we've got left is to smooth out those obtuse angles and make them into curves. There's one at your waist point, and the one you just made in the previous step. Take your curve tool and lay it down alongside one of those pesky angles. Slide the curve around until you find a section of it that fits nicely into the angle. The edge of the hip curve should be *touching* your line at points a few inches (or less) to each side of the angle.

Following the curve, draw a line between the two points. Be generous; you want your seam line to be one smooth, continuous curve, not two straight lines connected with a tiny bend. Erase or mark out the old line. Repeat for the other angle.

15. ADD SEAM ALLOWANCE
The last step is to add your ½" (or ⅝") SA. You know how it's done!

- - - - - - - - - - - - - - - - - - -

`Tip:` I like to add a full inch of SA
along the bottom hip line, so I can do
a ¹/₂" double-turned hem. Think about
how you plan to hem your shirt, and add
your SA accordingly. Another part of
the pattern where a different size of
SA is generally used is the neckline.
Because it is such a small curved
area, we usually use only a ¹/₄" SA
to minimize distortion.

- - - - - - - - - - - - - - - - - - -

16. CHECK YOUR WORK
Your first piece of the shirt pattern is now nearly finished, but before you cut it out, let's do a quick once-over:

* Did you double-check that all six corners (CF neck, high shoulder point, shoulder point, top of side seam, bottom of side seam, CF hip) are right angles?

* Did you check that there aren't any other pointy bits aside from those six corners?

* Does the basic shape of the shirt look right to you?

17. CUT IT OUT
We still have the 2" of blank space we added in step 2, and now we will define the top and bottom edges on it. Draw a line, the full length of your shirt, ½" to the left of CF and parallel to it. Place notches at the top and bottom of this line to indicate where the

make the back shirt

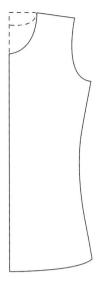

step 2

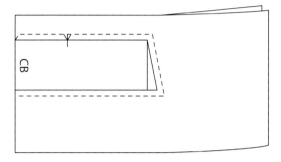

make the collar

steps 1–3

placket will be folded back. Fold your pattern on this line, which is the edge of the placket. With the paper still folded, go ahead and cut out your entire front shirt, so that the top and bottom of the placket area will mirror the neckline and hemline.

Make the Back Shirt

1. Prepare your paper

Get a piece of paper at least as big as your front pattern piece, placket still folded back. Lay your front pattern on top of it, lining up CF (*not* the fold) with the left-side edge of the new piece, which will be CB (there obviously will be no need for a placket on the back of your shirt). Trace around the shirt front to establish most of the back pattern. The only area that will be different is the neckline. After tracing the outer edges, you can also trace your shoulder line and HSP onto the back pattern piece. If you like, you can also trace the other seam lines from the front, but this is optional.

2. Plot the back neckline

Using the front neckline as reference, draw a ¼" line from HSP down, perpendicular to the shoulder seam. Back neck drops, especially when a collar is involved, are pretty small, generally from ½" to 1". I would recommend using 1" for now; you can always adjust it later, if necessary. Draw a line from HSP over to CB, perpendicular of course, and measure your back neck drop down from there. Then draw the back neckline, making sure it also hits CB at a 90° angle, and that it meets the shoulder seam (also at a right angle) at the exact same point as the front neckline.

3. Add seam allowance and cut

Add ¼" SA to your new back neckline. You can now cut out your back pattern piece.

Make the Collar

1. Prepare your paper

Start with a piece of paper that measures 6" wide and twice your full neck width in length. Fold the paper in half crosswise (so the shorter ends meet). Orient the fold to your left; this is CB.

2. Plot the points

To determine the length of your collar, you'll need to measure the exact length of your combined front and back neck seam lines from your shirt pattern pieces, from CF to CB. Use your tape measure, as it will allow you to measure along the curves of your neck seam lines. Do not include any seam allowances in your measurement. Use this measurement to plot a perpendicular line out from CB, about an inch down from the top edge of your paper. Draw a parallel line 3" down from the first line. Connect the two lines with a 3" perpendicular line. Now we can add a bit of shape to the collar points. Extend the bottom line ½" past the end, and connect this point to the top line. This gives a slightly less square look to the collar. We can play more with collar shapes later on, but for now you've got a basic collar pattern.

3. Add seam allowance and cut

Add ¼" SA to the three drawn sides of the pattern. Along the top line of the collar, which will be the neck seam, mark the length of your back neck seam line with a notch, measuring out from CB. This notch indicates

make the sleeve

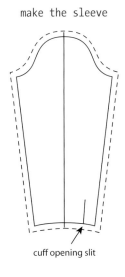

cuff opening slit

step 8

where the collar will match up with the intersecting shoulder seam. Also notch CB. Cut out your collar, still folded, and open it up for the full pattern piece.

Make the Sleeve

The process of drafting the sleeve for a button-down is exactly the same as for the T-shirt, only the measurements will be different to accommodate more ease in the woven fabric. So if you already made a knit sleeve pattern, this will all sound familiar . . .

1. Prepare your paper

Get a piece of paper that is 4" longer than your sleeve length measurement and 4" wider than your full bicep circumference. Fold the paper in half lengthwise, and keep the folded edge on your left. We'll be drafting half of the sleeve and then unfolding the paper to get a whole sleeve pattern.

2. Plot the length and wrist

Along the fold, make a mark about 2" down from the top of your paper. From this point, measure down the length of your sleeve,

minus 1" for the cuff, and make another mark. From here, hold your ruler perpendicular to the fold and draw a line that measures your half-wrist circumference, plus ½" for the cuff overlap.

3. Make the cap

The sleeve cap is the curve at the top of your sleeve, which is shaped like a bell. Before we can draft the cap, we'll need to determine our cap height. I use a formula of two-thirds (.67) times armhole height. So if you used an armhole height of 8", your cap height will be 5⅜" (I rounded to the nearest eighth of an inch). Measure down this height from the top mark on your paper. From this point, draw a line, perpendicular to the fold, that measures your half-bicep circumference. Connect this bicep point with your wrist point; this is the underarm seam line. OK, now we're ready to draft that bell-shaped cap! Start by establishing a 90° angle (from the fold) at the top point of your sleeve; just draw a short ½" line or so. Then hold the ruler perpendicular to the underarm seam line, and draw another ½" line toward the fold. Now connect these two short lines by curving downward from the top one and curving upward from the lower one, meeting in a very smooth S curve. Make sure that where the two opposing curves meet, the transition is seamless (see diagram). It should almost be a straight line for about an inch or two.

4. Check the sleeve cap

The seam line you just created for your sleeve cap will be sewn to the armhole of your shirt, so we must make sure the two lines fit together. Measure the exact length of your sleeve cap seam line, and measure the length along your armhole curve (not the straight armhole height), excluding SA. Compare the two measurements. If they are equal, or if the

sleeve cap seam is up to ½" bigger than the armhole, you're in good shape. But if the sleeve cap is *smaller* than the armhole, you'll have to adjust it until they are at least equal. You can increase the cap seam length by lowering your bicep line, increasing your bicep width, or beefing up the upper part of the curve (see diagram). Play around with it until the two measurements match, or the sleeve cap is slightly bigger (this bit of ease will give the cap some shaping to cup your shoulder).

5. Square the wrist corner

Down at the wrist point, extend the underarm seam line by about 1", then hold your ruler perpendicular to it. Slide the ruler up and down, until it intersects the wrist line about two-thirds of the way over from the fold. Draw a line from the extended underarm seam line to the wrist line.

6. Smooth the wrist line

Using your curve tool, blend the obtuse angle you just made in the wrist line so that it is a nice smooth curve. Be careful not to affect either of the two right angles at the ends of the wrist.

7. Add seam allowance

Add ½" (or ⅝") SA to the cap curve, underarm seam, and wrist line.

8. Cut it out

With the paper still folded, cut out the sleeve, being careful not to let the underside slide around while you're cutting. Once your sleeve is cut out, make a mark along the wrist seam line, halfway between the center line of the sleeve and the underarm seam line on the right side. From this mark, draw a perpendicular line extending 3" up from the wrist line (see diagram). This will be the slit at the cuff opening.

make the cuff

steps 1-2

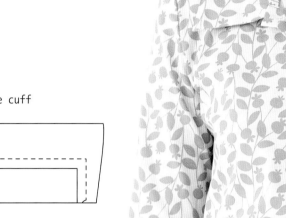

MAKE THE CUFF

1. PLOT THE LENGTH AND WIDTH

Get a small piece of paper, at least 6" by (your wrist measurement plus 2"), and fold it lengthwise. Place the fold at the bottom. Along the fold, plot your wrist length, plus 1" for overlap. We'll be making a 2" cuff, so draw a line 2" up and parallel to the fold. Draw two lines from the wrist points up to the line, at 90°, so you have a rectangle.

2. ADD SEAM ALLOWANCE

Ignoring the fold, add SA to the three drawn lines. Notch at the fold points, and there's your cuff!

3. LABEL AND TRUE YOUR PIECES

All that's left is to label all of your pieces with CF/CB, grain line, name of the garment, name of the pattern piece (front and back shirt, sleeve, cuff, and collar) and cutting instructions (front shirt is "cut 2," back is "cut 1 on fold," sleeve is "cut 2," cuff is "cut 2," and collar is "cut 2"). Check that all corresponding pieces match along seam lines.

SEWING INSTRUCTIONS: Sew fronts to back at shoulder and side seams, using **French seams**. Stitch the two collar pieces together (right sides facing) along the three outer edges, turn right-side out, press, and edgestitch from the right side. Sew the collar to neckline, matching CB and CF, and finish the neck seam with a bias-tape (or ¼" **self-bias**) binding. Press ½" under at placket edge, and fold the placket, so right sides are facing, at notches. Stitch across neck edge for ½" extension. Turn the placket right-side out and press. From inside, edgestitch along the inner folded placket edge. Sew the underarm seams of sleeves with French seams. Finish the slit with a ¼" self-bias binding (see Insider Sewing Techniques, page 148). Fold cuffs lengthwise, with right sides facing, and stitch the two short ends. Turn right side out and press. Lay the cuff on the right side of sleeve, with raw edges together, and seam one long side of the cuff to the sleeve. Flip the cuff and tuck ½" of the cuff facing and all SA inside of cuff seam; press. Edgestitch around all four sides of the cuff, from the right side. Hem your shirt with a double-turned ½" hem. Stitch buttonholes onto CF placket and cuffs, and sew on your buttons.

p. 9

Shirt Variation 1: BETSY JACKET

We can use our Basic Shirt pattern (page 58) as the basis for a cute, lightweight spring jacket, with big buttons and a gathered waistline. Try it in denim, canvas, corduroy, or any jacket-weight fabric. (Note: If you made your shirt pattern with a snug fit, you may want to grade it up a size or two to make the jacket; see Throw a Fit, page 134). Decide in advance the length you want your jacket, and how far down from HSP the waist seam will be. You'll need several medium-sized pieces of paper for this pattern.

1. MAKE THE UPPER FRONT

Trace the top half of your shirt front from page 60, from the waist line up, onto a new piece of paper, and transfer the CF line. Draw a line where you want the gathered waist seam, perpendicular to CF (I put mine 14" down from HSP). Add SA to the waist seam line. Lower and/or widen the neckline as desired, including ¼" SA before you trim anything away from the neck. I made my neck width 9" (so the half-neck width is 4½") and my drop 4¼". We are going to put a wider, separate 2" placket on this jacket, so we'll also need to trim away the original fold-back placket and a little more. Draw a parallel line, ½" to the right of CF, and cut on this line.

2. MAKE THE UPPER BACK

Follow the same steps to make the back pattern, except for the placket adjustment (you'll just stick with good ol' CB). Be sure the back neckline matches up with the front at the shoulder seams. True the back to the front at the shoulder and side seams.

3. MAKE THE RUFFLE

Measure the width of the waist seam line (including SA), and multiply this number by 1.5. Draft a rectangle this wide by however long you want the ruffle part of the jacket (I used 7"), plus 1½" for SA. This piece can be the front and back ruffle, though the back one will be cut on the fold.

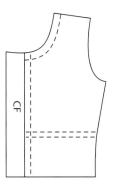

step 1

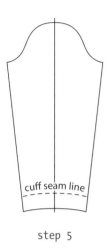

cuff seam line

step 5

4. MAKE THE PLACKET PIECE

Measure the length of the front edge of the jacket (excluding SA), and add it to the length of the ruffle (excluding SA). Add 1" SA to this number. Draft a rectangle this long, by 5" wide (2 times the 2" placket + ½" SA for each side). Fold the rectangle in half lengthwise, and notch the short sides at the fold.

5. MAKE THE SLEEVE

You can shorten the Basic Shirt sleeve to three-quarter length, or leave it long. Either way, make a cuff by measuring up evenly 1½" (or your preferred cuff height) from the cuff seam line, and cutting on this line. Add SA to each side of the edges you just cut.

6. LABEL AND TRUE YOUR PATTERN PIECES

Label your pattern pieces with CF and/or CB, grain line, your style name, the name of each pattern piece (upper front and back, front/back ruffle, placket, sleeve, and cuff), size or key measurements, and cutting instructions (the upper front is "cut 2," upper back is "cut 1 on fold," front ruffle is "cut 2," back ruffle [same pattern piece as front ruffle] is "cut 1 on fold," the sleeves are "cut 2," and the cuffs are "cut 4"). Check that all corresponding pieces match along seam lines.

SEWING INSTRUCTIONS: Sew upper fronts to back along the side and shoulder seams. Finish the seams with an overedge zigzag or bias binding. Sew the ruffle fronts to ruffle back along the side seams, and finish. Run two rows of gathering stitches along the top edge of your ruffle, gather and stitch to upper body, making sure to line up the ruffle side seams with the jacket side seams. Finish this seam, and edgestitch from the right side, if desired. Hem the bottom edge of the ruffle with a double-turned ½" hem. Finish the neck edge with a bias tape or self-bias facing (see Insider Sewing Techniques, page 148).

Fold the placket piece lengthwise, right sides facing, and stitch the two short seams. Turn the placket right-side out and press. With right sides together, stitch one side of the placket piece to one side of the front. Flip, tuck in all SAs, and press. From inside, baste the placket closed along the seam line. From the outside, edgestitch the placket and remove basting. Repeat for the other side of placket. Sew underarm seams of sleeves and finish. Fold all four cuff pieces, right sides together, and seam the short ends. Press the seams open. With right sides facing, seam cuffs to their facings along cuff edge. Turn right sides out, press, and edgestitch. Seam the outer edge of cuff to sleeve, flip, tuck in all SAs, and press. From inside, baste the cuff facing along seam line. From the outside, edgestitch the cuff and remove basting. Set the sleeves into the armholes. Complete with buttonholes and buttons, slip your new jacket on, and go out for a drink. You deserve it!

Shirt Variation 2: STELLA BLOUSE

For this sweet pullover version of the button-down shirt, we'll add a pintucked bib placket, a mandarin collar, and some shirring at the front and sleeve caps. I used a lovely iridescent cotton voile for mine; pick out your own favorite lightweight woven for yours. You'll need two pieces of paper about the size of your Basic Shirt patterns from page 76, and at least as long, plus one a few inches wider than your sleeve, and some smaller scraps.

1. MAKE THE FRONT SHIRT

Establish a line or edge at the left side of your paper, and lay the left placket edge of your front shirt pattern from page 78 on this line. Trace around the pattern, and transfer the CF line onto the new pattern. Enlarge the neckline slightly by removing the ¼" SA line, so the old seam line will now be the SA line. Draw a rectangle the size

you'd like (half of) your placket to be. Cut out the rectangle and set it aside (it will become the placket pattern). Add SA to the placket seam edges you just cut.

Note: The extension that was the placket will now become shirring under the placket seam. The left-side edge is now CF and will be cut on the fold.

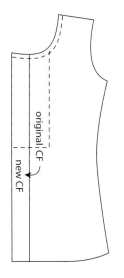

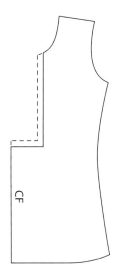

step 1

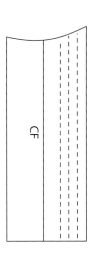

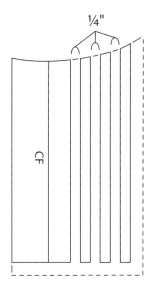

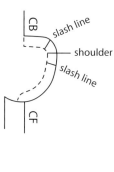

step 2

step 4

2. MAKE THE PLACKET

Draw three evenly spaced lines where you want to add your pintucks, leaving at least an inch between the first tuck and CF. Cut on these lines, and lay all four pieces on a scrap of paper, spread apart, with ¼" of space at each tuck. Tape all the pieces down securely. Connect the neckline and bottom edge line across the tuck spaces, and add SA to the bottom and right side of the placket piece. The original placket is retained along the left side of CF. Notch each side of each tuck, at top and bottom edges, as well as where the placket folds back.

3. MAKE THE BACK SHIRT

The back pattern piece can be exactly the same as the Basic Shirt back from page 80, or you can add a bit of shirring at the back neck by simply adding a 1½" extension to CB. Enlarge the neckline by ¼" all around as with the front.

4. MAKE THE MANDARIN COLLAR

On a scrap of paper, trace the front neck seam line (*not* the seam allowance line) of your Basic Shirt pattern from page 78, including the front button placket extension, marking CF and about 1" of the shoulder seam. Then lay the Basic Shirt back piece, matching it to the front at the shoulder seam, and draw the back neckline as one continuous curve (eliminating both SAs at shoulder). Mark CB. Now plot a series of points 1" toward the center of the curve, and connect the points into a parallel curved line. Connect the two curves at CB with a perpendicular line. Do the same at the front edge, but round the top corner of the collar, if you like. Now, to open up the tight curve of the collar at the shoulder seam, and let it stand up slightly, draw three slash lines (one at the shoulder seam and one about 1" to each side of it) (see diagram). Cut on each line, starting at the collar edge and cutting toward the neck seam, but leaving ⅛" attached at the seam line. Spread each cut apart by about ⅛"–3⁄16", and tape paper behind. Smooth out the curves if necessary, and add ¼" SA all around collar, except for the CB line, which will be cut on the fold. Notch CB and shoulder point.

5. MAKE THE SLEEVE

On a folded piece of paper, with the fold on the left side, draw a parallel line 1" to the right of the fold. Lay your folded Basic Shirt sleeve pattern (page 81) with the fold on this line, and trace around the cap, underarm seam, and cuff. Extend the lines at the cap and cuff to meet the fold. Shorten the pattern to be a three-quarter-length sleeve, if desired, leaving a 1" SA. Cut the sleeve pattern out while folded, and notch the cap at fold.

6. LABEL AND TRUE YOUR PATTERN PIECES

Label your pattern pieces with CF and/or CB, grain line, your style name, the name of each pattern piece (front and back blouse, front placket, collar, and sleeve), size or key measurements, and cutting instructions (the front and back blouse pieces are "cut 1 on fold," the front placket is "cut 2," the collar is "cut 2 on fold," and the sleeve is "cut 2"). Check that all corresponding pieces match along seam lines.

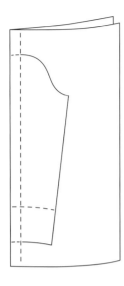

step 5

SEWING INSTRUCTIONS: Stitch all pintucks by matching notches and sewing ⅛" from the fold. Press the tucks away from CF. Press under ½" of the placket, and press again on the fold line. From inside, edgestitch along the inner placket fold. On the blouse front piece, **stay-stitch** (with fairly small stitches) the two lower corners where the placket will be inserted, exactly on the seam line, and clip corners almost to the stitch line. Run two rows of gathering stitches along the lower edge of the placket seam. Gather to fit the placket, and pin placket in place, overlapping the bottom edges at CF. Stitch around sides and bottom of placket, and finish the raw edge with a bias binding or overedge zigzag. Sew the front to the back along shoulder and side seams, with French seams. With right sides facing, sew the top edge of collar, turn right-side out, press, and edgestitch. (If you added shirring to the back neck, run your gathering stitches and gather it up now.) With right sides facing, stitch outer neck edge of collar to neckline, flip up and tuck

facing edge and all SAs inside of collar, press, and baste from the inside. Edgestitch the seam from the outside, and remove basting. Sew the underarm seams of sleeves with French seams, and run two rows of gathering stitches across top 4" of sleeve cap. Gather and set sleeves into armholes. Finish the seam with a bias binding or overedge zigzag. Hem the cuff and bottom hems of your blouse with a double-turned ½" hem. Add your buttonholes and buttons to complete, and admire your handiwork!

All Dressed Up

Dresses may go in and out of fashion, but what I love most about them is that they make for a one-step outfit. All you need is a dress and you're, well, dressed!

Essentially, a dress is not so different from a shirt; it's just longer. So you can take almost any of the T-shirt or blouse patterns we've made thus far, lengthen them, and voilà— you've got dresses! Who knew it could be that easy? This is the simplest way to begin a dress pattern, provided you already have a knit or woven top pattern that is similar to the top half of the dress you want to make. Just alter the bodice area as you wish to suit your design, then add the skirt area, which can be a one-piece continuation of the bodice or a separate skirt pattern piece, with a seam at the waist or hip. You can also do the reverse: Start with a skirt pattern that you love, and build it up from there, or combine a skirt pattern with a top pattern to make the perfect dress. Isn't it fun being a designer? The possibilities are mind-boggling when you can make anything you dream up!

BASIC DRESS

I find that a simple, strappy shift dress is an endlessly versatile style to have on hand in your pattern library as the basis for all kinds of options: printed cotton summer sundresses, fancy silk satin cocktail dresses, casual corduroy jumpers . . . you get the idea. The variety will come from the fabrication and details. So get out your paper and pencil—we've got a dress to draft! You'll need three pieces of paper: two that measure about 2" wider than your quarter-bust and 2" longer than your **bodice** length, and one that measures about 2" wider than your quarter-sweep and 2" longer than your skirt. (Subtract the "waist down from HSP" measurement from your total dress length to determine the skirt length.)

MEASUREMENTS

Length (HSP to hem)

Waist down from HSP (where you want the waist seam)

Front bodice height* (up from waist seam)

Back bodice height* (up from waist seam)

Neck width (distance between straps) front and back

Bust**

Waist** (at seam)

Hip** (at widest)

Sweep circumference** (must be at least several inches bigger than hip)

*Because this dress has straps, it doesn't go all the way up to the shoulder. Therefore you will need to decide where you want the top edge of the dress to be. You've already decided where the waist seam will be, so measure up from that line to determine the bodice height. You may want a shaped neckline across the top; if so, you can determine a "high" and "low" bodice height measurement. You also may want a lower bodice height in back, so determine that now as well. Or, just keep the whole thing straight across; you can always go

back and make a more advanced neckline later.

**Add 1" ease to each of these measurements and divide the total by 4. These will be referred to as quarter-bust, quarter-waist, etc.

1. PLOT THE WAIST LINE

Establish a CF line or edge at the left side of your paper. Near the bottom of your paper, from CF, plot a perpendicular line that equals your quarter-waist measurement. (Remember: This is where you want the seam of the dress to sit, not necessarily your true waistline. You may want to raise it up to just below the bust for an **empire waist**, or have it nearer your true waist. For the purposes of this exercise I wouldn't use a **dropped waistline**, as it requires a different kind of shaping through the waist area.)

2. DRAFT THE NECKLINE

Now measure up from the waist your front bodice height, and mark along CF. If you are planning a shaped neckline, mark the lower of your two heights for now. From CF, plot a perpendicular line that measures your quarter-bust. Connect this bust point to the waist point, forming the side seam. Square the bottom corner, where the

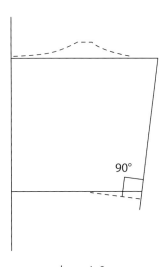

steps 1–2

side seam meets your waist, which will cause your waist line to curve slightly downward. Next you can sketch out your neckline if you want to shape it, so along the bust line, mark your neck width. Here you can add in the higher bodice height if you measured one, and draw in the shape you envision. I would suggest keeping it simple for your first dress, and not varying your bodice height more than an inch or so, until you have a bit more experience with how the **flat pattern** translates to the body. On the other hand, we are going to do a little experiment in a moment, so if your heart is set on a curvy neckline, go for it now, and we'll test it before going any further.

3. ADD BUST SHAPING AND CHECK NECKLINE

Most of us will require some darts to add a little shaping around the bust and make the dress fit better. There are two ways to go about adding darts. The first way is what we did for the skirt pattern: Basically, we guessed at the size and placement of the darts, to be fine-tuned when fitting the muslin. That works fine for the skirt, but bust shapes vary so much that I prefer to use the

following method in this situation. Trace your front bodice pattern onto a folded piece of muslin (placing CF on the fold), either using dressmaker's carbon or, if your muslin is sheer enough, you can simply lay it on top of the pattern and trace with pencil. Cut out the muslin bodice, adding at least ½" of seam allowance as you cut. Don't worry, the SA doesn't need to be perfect for now; we just need a little extra space in case we need to adjust our lines. Wearing a slim-fitting T-shirt or tank, place the waistline of the bodice where you want it on your body, and pin it to your shirt. (Safety pins work great for this as they can't fall out or poke you!) Next, begin pinning the rest of the bodice to your T-shirt. You will probably have a hard time getting it to lie flat, because *you* are probably not flat! So, working on one side only, form one or two darts around the bust, ending at either the neckline or side seam. Pinch the darts (toward the outside is fine) where you see the fullness naturally forming at the edges of the pattern, and pin them until you are satisfied. Once you have one side completed, do your best to replicate the darts on the other side (mirror-imaged) so you can see the overall fit. Check if you need to adjust

the neck or side seam lines to smooth them out where the darts occur; you want gentle curves or lines, not points! Mark your darts and any adjustments with a pencil right on the muslin. You can also now examine the shape of your neckline, and adjust it, if desired.

4. ADJUST THE PATTERN

After making sure that you have marked all your darts and line adjustments clearly in pencil on the muslin, take out the pins and lay it flat on top of your original paper pattern. Transfer the marks from muslin to paper, with a pushpin or carbon paper, cleaning them up, if necessary. Dart legs should be straight lines and should meet in a clear point. Once this is complete, go ahead and add your SA for real. Then you can cut the pattern out, remembering first to fold and place a bit of tape on the darts before you cut, pushing the dart allowance toward CF on vertical darts, and down on horizontal ones.

5. MAKE THE BACK BODICE

Repeat the waistline, neckline, and side seam steps, making the neckline as you

want it in the back. Most often, the back neckline of this type of dress is just a straight line across from side seam to side seam, but you can give it a little shaping if you want to. Just be sure that the length of the side seams for the back pattern is exactly the same as the side seams on the front pattern (with darts folded if they end in the side seam), since they will be sewn together! There will be no need for darts on the back bodice.

6. MAKE THE STRAP

You can either use self-fabric straps, or make them out of a trim like ribbon or twill tape. If you plan to use a trim, you might just make a note of the strap length needed on one of the other pattern pieces. If you want to make the straps out of the same fabric as the rest of the dress, you'll need a pattern piece. To determine strap length, you'll need to subtract your front bodice height from the "waist down from HSP" measurement, and write down the number. Then do the same with your back bodice height. Add these two numbers together, and that will be your finished strap length. Add an additional 2" for seam allowance (1" at each end) so you have a little extra length in case you need to adjust. For the width, you'll need four times your desired finished strap width. So if you want ¼" straps, your pattern should be 1" wide. Notch the front and back bodice patterns where you intend to place the straps. You may want to consider bra strap placement if you want the dress straps to hide your bra straps. I also like to make my straps closer together in the back than in the front, as this helps keep them from slipping off my shoulders.

7. MAKE THE FRONT/BACK SKIRT

On your large piece of paper, establish CF/CB along the left side. Make a mark 2" up from the bottom edge, and from this point draft a line perpendicular to CF/CB that equals your quarter sweep measurement. Measure up from this line your skirt length, and plot another line the same length as (and parallel to) the first. Connect the endpoints of these two lines to form the side seam. Believe it or not, this rectangle is all you need for both the front and back skirt pattern to your dress. The skirt will be shirred into the waistline of the bodice; the wider your sweep, the more shirring you will have at the waist. Be sure it's big enough to comfortably accommodate your hips. To finish, add SA all around, adding accordingly at the hemline for the type of hem you want to use. One inch is a good standard hem allowance. Cut out the skirt pattern piece.

8. LABEL AND TRUE YOUR PATTERN PIECES

The final step is to label your pattern pieces with CF and/or CB, grain line, your style name (Super Cute Dress, or whatever you want to name it), the name of each pattern piece (front bodice, back bodice, front/back skirt, and strap if you made a pattern for it), size or key measurements, and cutting instructions (the bodice pieces are "cut 1 on fold," the straps are "cut 2," and the skirt is "cut 2 on fold"). Continue all dart legs out to the edge of your seam allowance, and notch the darts. Check that all corresponding pieces match along seam lines, especially the bodice side seams.

SEWING INSTRUCTIONS: Stitch the darts. Run two rows of gathering stitches along the top edge of each skirt piece. Gather and seam one to the front bodice, and one to the back. Finish the seam with an overedge zigzag stitch. Stitch the right-side seam with a French seam. On the left-side seam, insert an invisible zipper that extends from armpit to hip. Sew the lower half of the seam, and finish with a **mock-French finish**. To make the straps, fold and press straps down the center lengthwise, then fold edges in to meet center crease and press again. Pin, and edgestitch along both of the long sides. Baste the straps to the neckline, matching raw edges, and try on the dress. Adjust strap length and placement, if necessary. Also check if the hem length needs adjusting, and do so now. Use a bias-tape facing to finish the neckline, enclosing the strap ends in the process. Hem the dress with a double-turned ½" hem.

p.14

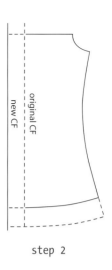

step 2

Dress Variation 1: Gertie Dress

Let's try a knit dress, based on one of our T-shirt patterns, the Marguerite (page 66). We'll add some shirring to the yoke seam and a long ruffle to lengthen it into a dress. (If you haven't made the Marguerite style yet, it's just a few quick adjustments to the Basic T pattern (page 58), so go ahead and do that first. Trust me, it'll only take a few minutes!) This'll look smashing in any lightweight solid or printed jersey.

1. Make the yoke

The yoke pattern piece will be used as is, and I'm choosing to eliminate the sleeve, but you can use it if you want to. You may want to make a copy of the yoke pattern to keep with the dress, or else you can make a note on the dress pattern or envelope to borrow the yoke from your Marguerite T. You will also need a back yoke pattern for this dress, which you may not have done for the T. If you don't have one, make it now, and make sure it is the same length as the front yoke. Decide the total length you want the dress to be, and of that, how long the ruffle will be.

2. Add shirring to the yoke seam

On a new piece of paper, a few inches wider than the pattern, establish CF/CB at left and draw a parallel line 2" to the right of it. Now place the front lower body pattern piece, so that CF is on the new line, and trace it. Extend the top (yoke) seam line and the hemline 2" to meet the new CF/CB. This will add a total of 4" of shirring to the yoke seam. Determine whether you need to lengthen this pattern piece, and do so now, if desired. I am making a long ruffle for my dress, 10", (and my T is pretty long, 22½") so I'm just adding a couple of inches. This pattern piece will be the front and back bodice of the dress.

3. Make the bottom ruffle

Decide how long you want the ruffle to be. Add a total of 1½" (for ½" SA at the top and 1" hem allowance at the bottom). This will be the height of your pattern piece. For the width, measure the hemline of your new extended bodice piece, and multiply by 1.25. Add ½" SA. This is the width of the ruffle pattern piece. Draw a rectangle measuring the height by the width, and label one of the short sides "CF/CB."

4. Label and true your pattern pieces

Finally, label your pattern pieces with CF and/or CB, grain line, your style name, the name of each pattern piece (front yoke, back yoke, front/back bodice, and front/back ruffle), size or key measurements, and cutting instructions (the yoke pieces are "cut 1 on fold," the front/back bodice is "cut 2 on fold," and the ruffle is "cut 2 on fold"). Check that all corresponding pieces match along seam lines.

Sewing instructions: Run two rows of gathering stitches along the top edges of the front and back bodices. Pull the gathering threads to fit the yokes, and sew the bodices to the yokes. Sew the shoulder and side seams. Finish the neckline and armholes with a fold-over elastic binding. Sew the ruffle pieces together along the side seams (short ends). Run two rows of gathering stitches along one of the long sides of the ruffle, and gather to fit the lower edge of the dress. Sew the ruffle to the dress, matching the side seams of the ruffle to the side seams of the dress. Try the dress on to see if the length needs adjusting, and hem with a double-turned ½" hem.

p. 10

Dress Variation 2: Miette Dress

Now let's do a woven dress using the Basic Shirt (page 76) as our foundation. We'll create a drawstring-gathered waist, add some length and fullness, eliminate the collar and button placket, and borrow the sleeves from the Stella Blouse (page 86). Mine is in a dusty blue linen, but feel free to use any woven with good drape. Ready?

1. Make the front dress

On a piece of paper a few inches longer than you want your dress to be and a few inches wider than your Basic Shirt pattern from page 78, establish CF and lay your Basic Shirt front piece so that its CF aligns with CF on the paper. The shirt's placket will hang over the edge of the paper. Make sure the shirt pattern is near the top of your paper, so you will have room to add the skirt area. Keeping the CF neckline of the shirt touching CF on your paper, rotate the lower end of the shirt pattern 2" out to the right, so that the distance between the CF on your paper and CF of the shirt is 2" apart at the bottom of the shirt. Place some weights on the pattern in this position, trace around the neckline, shoulder seam, armhole, side seams, and hem. Remove the shirt pattern. Extend the side seam line (and SA line) down to your desired dress length, and use your ruler to extend the hemline evenly to this length, following the original curve. Extend the hemline to the CF edge of your paper. Connect the underarm point with the hem point in a straight line, eliminating the waist shaping. Square the corners at underarm and hem points. Add 1" SA to the hem.

2. Adjust the neckline

The neckline of the shirt is pretty small and high because it was made for a collar. For this dress, which will pull on over the head, you'll want a lower and wider scoop neck. Adjust this now, making sure the circumference is big enough to slip easily over your head, and add ¼" SA.

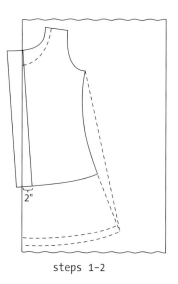

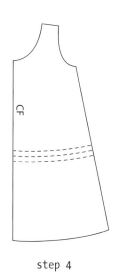

steps 1–2   step 4

3. Make the back dress

Trace the front pattern onto a new piece of paper and create a corresponding back neckline with ¼" SA.

4. Add the drawstring waist

Determine where you want the drawstring casing to sit, either on or below your true waist. Square a line out from CF at this point, and curve it slightly until it meets the side seam at a 90° angle. Check that this curve echoes the hemline curve. Now decide how wide you'd like the drawstring casing to be. Divide this number in half, and measure this distance above and below the curved line you drew, along the entire length of it, creating two new curved lines, which will be the seam lines of the casing.

5. Make the casing pattern

Whatever width you decided on for the casing (minimum 1"), add 1" SA (for ½" top and bottom). To determine the length, measure the center line that you drew for the waist (excluding side seam SA), and multiply it by 4. Draft a rectangle that measures the width (including SA) by the length. (The length doesn't need SA added because we want a little space between the casing ends to allow room for tying the drawstring.)

6. Make the drawstring pattern

Determine the length and width of your drawstring (remember, it should be at least a ½" narrower than the casing to slide through and gather easily). Add 1" SA to the length, and multiply the width by 4. Draft a rectangle with these measurements.

7. Make the sleeve

For the sleeve, either make a copy of the sleeve from the Stella Blouse (page 89) to keep with this pattern, or make a note on the envelope to borrow Stella's sleeve for this dress.

8. Label and true your pattern pieces

Label your pattern pieces with CF and/or CB, grain line, your style name, the name of each pattern piece (dress front, dress back, sleeve, drawstring casing, and drawstring), size or key measurements, and cutting instructions (the dress pieces are "cut 1 on fold," the sleeves are "cut 2," the casing and drawstring are "cut 1"). Check that all corresponding pieces match along seam lines.

SEWING INSTRUCTIONS: Stitch the shoulder and side seams with French seams. Hem the 2 short ends of the casing with a double-turned ¼" hem. Press the ½" SA under along both of the long sides. Pin the casing to the dress according to pattern markings, leaving a 1" gap at CF for the opening. Edgestitch along the top and bottom of the casing. Use premade or self-fabric bias tape to finish the neck edge with an inside facing. To make the sleeves, stitch the underarm seams (I'd use French seams for these, too). Run two rows of gathering stitches along the top half of the sleeve cap. Set the sleeves into the armholes. Finish the armhole seams with an overedge zigzag stitch or mock-French finish. Hem the sleeves with a double-turned ½" hem. Try on the dress, in case you need to adjust the length, and hem with a double-turned ½" hem.

Miss Fancy Pants

We all know how hard it is to find pants that fit, and how unflattering ill-fitting pants can be. Well, fret no more! Once you've made yourself a basic pant sloper, or base pattern, you'll have the foundation to making yourself dozens of variations on your favorite pant styles, from bloomers to bell-bottoms.

Be warned, however, that pants are by far the trickiest category of clothing to make patterns for. I definitely wouldn't tackle them until you've successfully made several of the other projects in this book. But pants may also be the category for which we most *need* to make our own patterns! There are so many converging measurements, angles, and curves below the belt that I'd dare to say no two bodies are exactly alike. So be prepared to make a couple of test muslins, and the extra work will be rewarded with your very first pair of custom-made trousers!

There are a few points you should consider before you begin your pant pattern. A good fit is the result of a finely tuned set of lines and curves, most of which can't be measured exactly from your body.

You probably have many pairs of pants with similar key measurements. But some just seem to fit "like a glove" and others languish in your closet unworn, due to barely perceptible differences that make them just not right. I'd strongly recommend that you take your tape measure to at least three pairs of pants that fit well and are roughly the style you have in mind. This can give you a valuable head start in drafting your first pattern, and eliminate much unnecessary trial and error.

Another important consideration is fabric choice. Most pants are made from wovens, because they are sturdy and tend to hold their shape better than knits. Wovens are generally divided into *top-weights* and *bottom-weights*. Top-weights are fabrics like poplin, voile, or batiste, essentially lighter-weight weaves you can picture making a great shirt or blouse. Bottom-weights include denim, corduroy, gabardine, or twill. These are easy to imagine as pants or skirts. This all may sound obvious when you think about it abstractly, but it's easy to lose sight of the best choice for your design when you are standing amid thousands of bolts of gorgeous cloth in every weight, color, and weave imaginable. It's best to think about what type of fabric will achieve the proper look for your pants before you even set foot in the fabric store, and you'll be glad you did.

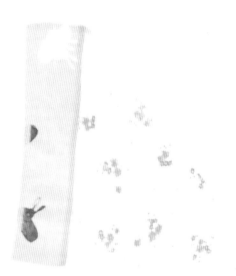

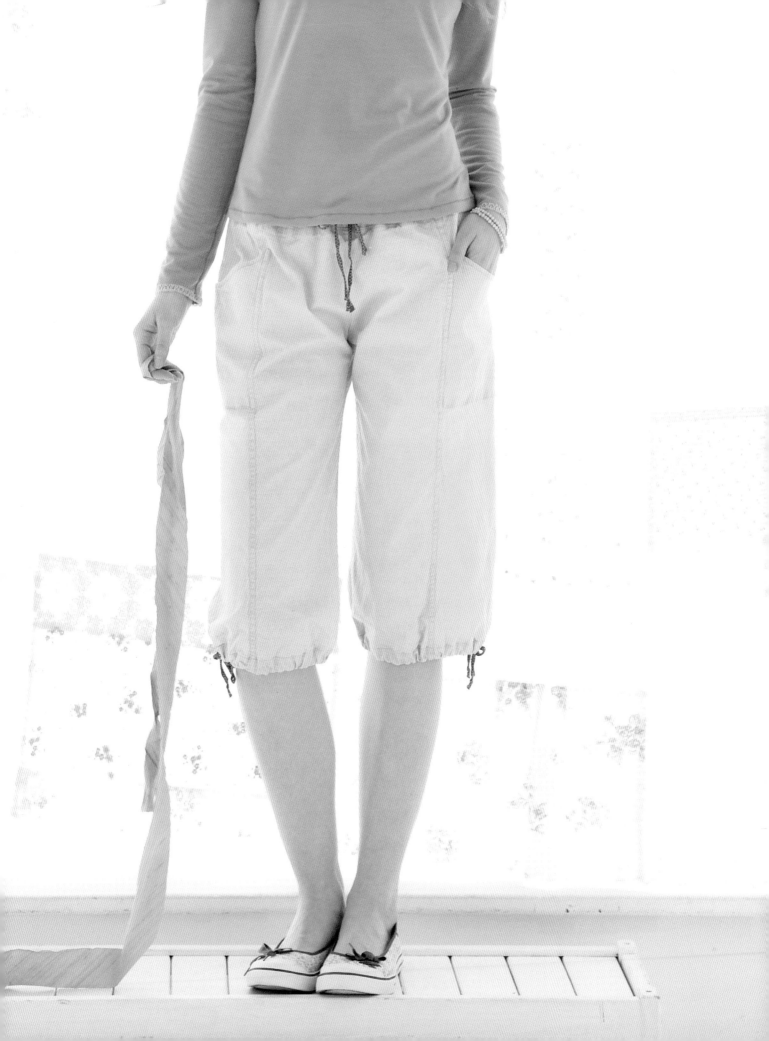

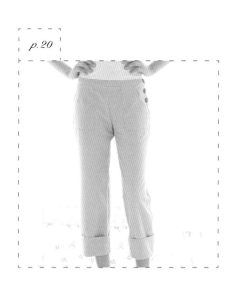

p. 20

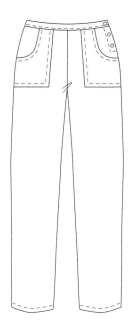

Basic Pant

A good simple pant that fits you could end up as your most prized pattern. And with slight adjustments in length, width, pockets, and waist treatments, you'll have a pair for every occasion. Once you've acquired a taste for couture, you just might never want to buy another pair of "off the rack" pants again! Most bottom-weight fabrics will work for these, such as denim, twill, canvas, or corduroy. To begin, you'll need a piece of paper that is 4–5" longer than your pant length, and 1.5 times your thigh circumference. We will be drafting both the front and back pant patterns simultaneously, since they have to work together.

Measurements

Length (waist to hem)

Waist* (where you want the pants to sit)

Hip*

Front hip** (side seam to side seam across front on hip line)

Back hip** (side seam to side seam across back on hip line)

Hip down from waist

Rise height

Thigh circumference⁺ (measure loosely, around 3–4" below the crotch)

Thigh down from waist

Knee circumference⁺ (also measure loosely, thinking of how loose the pants should be)

Knee down from waist

Cuff circumference⁺ (as with knee, envision the pants)

For each of these horizontal measurements, add 1" for ease, and divide the total by 4. These quarter measurements will be the ones you use for drafting the pattern. They will be referred to as quarter-waist, quarter-hip, etc.

**For each of these horizontal measurements, add ½" for ease, and divide in half. These will be referred to as half-knee, half-front hip, etc.*

⁺For your thigh, knee, and cuff circumferences, it'd be smart to take your measuring tape to a couple favorite pairs of pants, as the measurements may vary dramatically (more than you think) from your actual leg size.*

1. Plot the waist line and pant length

Draw a vertical line down the center of the entire length of your paper. Now draw two more parallel lines at ½" and 1" to the right of the first line. These three lines form the two seam allowances along the side seam and divide your front and back pattern pieces, as they will be drafted at the same time. To the left of the lines will be your back pattern piece, and to the right will be your front. Thus, all measurements for the back should begin at the leftmost of these three lines (the back side-seam line), and all measurements for the front should begin at the rightmost of the three lines (the front side-seam line). Make a cross-mark 3" down from the top edge, and square a line out to either side, across the full width of your paper; this is your waist line. Measure down from your waist line the length of your pant, and square out a line; this is your cuff hem line.

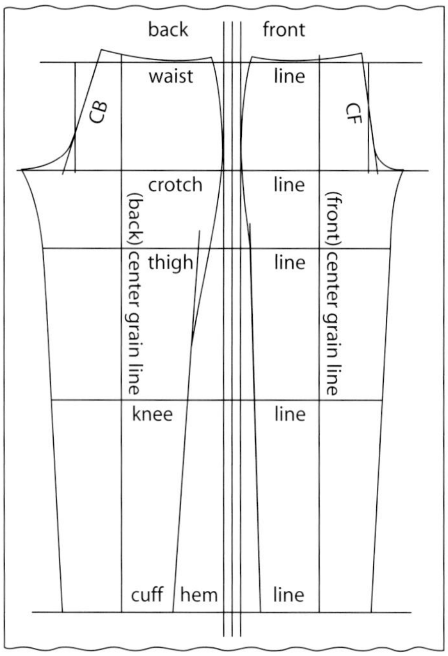
back
front
waist
line
CB
CF
crotch
line
(back) center grain line
(front) center grain line
thigh
line
knee
line
cuff
hem
line

steps 1–9

2. Plot the rise height

From the top cross-mark, measure down the length of your **rise** height and make another mark. Draft a line, perpendicular to the side-seam lines, measuring out to the left your half back hip measurement, and to the right your half front hip measurement. This is the crotch line. Square a line up from each of these points, to your waist line.

3. Make the crotch extensions

I wish I had a more elegant name for this step, but there's just no other way to say it! The crotch is what separates a pant into two tubes, differentiating it from a skirt. We need to create an extension on each side, so that each leg of the pants can wrap around one of your legs. To figure out the length of the back crotch extension, multiply your half back hip by .3, and extend the crotch line out by this number. For example, my half back hip is 11¼", so I extended the back hip line by 3⅜", for a total back crotch line of 14⅝". To figure out the front extension, multiply your half front hip by .25 and extend the crotch line accordingly.

4. Shape the back rise seam line

From the upper left corner of the back pant pattern (where the waist line meets the rise line), measure up 1" and over to the right 1¾", and make a mark. Now find the halfway point on your back rise seam, and make a mark ½" below it. Take your ruler and connect these two marks, continuing the line down to the crotch line. Then, using your hip curve, draw a curve from the crotch point (tip of crotch extension) to the point where the new angled line intersects the old vertical line.

5. Shape the front rise seam line

From the upper right corner of your front pant pattern (where the waist line meets the rise line), measure up ¼", and over to the left ½", and make a mark. Now find the halfway point along the front rise line, and make a mark ¼" above it. Connect these two marks with the ruler, again continuing the line down to the crotch line. Make a slight curve to connect the crotch point up to the new angled rise seam line, blending into it well below the halfway mark.

6. Shape the waist line and side seams

At each of the two top points of your new angled rise seams (which happen to be CF and CB), square a line out (toward the side seams) about ½". Blend these ½" lines to the waist line in gentle, very slight curves. Along each of your new curved waist seam lines, measure your quarter-waist measurement from CF and CB, toward your side seams, and mark. These points will tell you how much to shape your side seams.

Note: **When you do this, if your quarter-waist measurement meets, or goes beyond, the side-seam line [on either front or back], go back and slightly decrease the angle of the corresponding rise seam line.**

Along your side-seam lines, measure down your hip down from waist measurement, and mark. Using the hip curve, draw a slight curve to connect the hip points to the waist points, and square the top corners, if necessary.

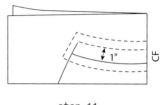

step 11

7. ESTABLISH THE CENTER GRAIN LINES

Along the crotch line of each side (front and back), find the halfway point between the crotch point and side seam lines, and mark. From each of these marks, draw a line up and down, parallel to the side seam lines, from waist to hem.

8. PLOT THE THIGH, KNEE, AND CUFF WIDTHS

Along the center grain line, measure your thigh down from waist measurement and mark. Square a line out to either side from this point. On this thigh line, from each side of center, measure out *one-half* of your half-thigh circumference measurement, and mark. Along the center grain line, measure your knee down from waist measurement and mark. Square a line out to either side from this point. On this knee line, from each side of center, measure out *one-half* of your half-knee circumference measurement, and mark. On the bottom hemline, do the same with your half-cuff circumference.

9. DRAW THE SIDE SEAMS AND INSEAMS

With your ruler, or a yardstick if you have one handy, connect the cuff points to the knee points, and on to the thigh points, and continue the lines up to the crotch line (for the **inseam**) and hip point (for the side seam). Smooth the angles into a nice, smooth, subtle curve. Along the inseam, be sure that the line meets the bottom of the rise seam (at crotch line) at a right angle. Along the side seam, your new seam line should gently blend from the thigh point up to the original side seam line, at or near (below) the hip point.

10. ADD SEAM ALLOWANCE

Now you can add your SA to all sides of the pattern. The original SA lines you drew in step 1 will become curved to reflect your new side seam lines; the original lines were just to allow space so you don't have to tape paper on now. You'll probably want to add a full 1" of SA at the cuff, to allow for a double-turned ½" hem, but if you have other plans you can add your SA accordingly.

11. MAKE THE WAISTBAND

If your hips are pretty straight, or you made your pants on the high-waisted side, you can make a straight waistband, as described in the sidebar of the skirt chapter. But if you're a curvier gal, or your pants will be sitting somewhere south of your belly button, proceed as follows: Lay your front pant pattern on a folded scrap of paper that's at least as wide as the pattern. Align the front rise seam (CF) on the fold of the paper (the seam allowance will be hanging over the fold). Transfer the waist and about the top 2" of the side seam lines to your paper, by poking holes through the pattern with a pin, about ½" apart. Remove the pattern and fill in the line with your pencil. Now, along the waist line of your pant pattern, measure up 1" in several spots, to make a parallel curved line. Extend the side seam line up to meet the top of waistband, following its same angle. Add SA along the top and bottom edges and side seam, and cut it out while still folded. Label and notch CF.

step 13

Repeat with your back pant to make the back waistband piece. On the back piece, we also need to add a button extension to one side, so extend the waistband out by an additional 1" (plus SA). Cut out both waistband pieces with the paper folded. On the back piece, cut off the 1" extension on one side only, so the pattern piece is not symmetrical. Label and notch CB, and notch where the extension begins.

12. MAKE THE FLY EXTENSION PIECE
In order to close this pant with buttons, we'll need an underlap extension. On a small scrap of paper, make a rectangle that measures 3" wide (1" doubled + ½" SA + ½" SA) by the length you'd like your fly (4–5" should do it) + ½" SA + ½" SA.

13. MAKE THE PATCH POCKET
On a scrap of paper, a bit bigger than you want your pocket to be, trace the upper portion of your front pant pattern. Using the waist line and side seam as two of the sides, draft a rectangular pocket to your liking, and draw a curved line across the upper left corner, toward the side seam, to be the pocket opening. Remember to make it big enough for your hand to slip inside! (Lay your hand on the paper as a guideline.) Also be sure to make the opening low enough that it doesn't interfere with the button placket. Add SA to the opening, right, and bottom edges of the

pocket piece; the top (waist) and left (side seam) sides already have it.

14. LABEL AND TRUE YOUR PATTERN PIECES
Label your pattern pieces with CF and/or CB, grain line, your style name, the name of each pattern piece (front and back pant, front and back waistband, underlap, and pocket), size or key measurements, and cutting instructions (front and back pant pieces are "cut 2," front and back waistband are "cut 2," underlap is "cut 2," and pocket is "cut 2"). Check that all corresponding pieces match along seam lines. This will be especially important in this case, because you drafted the two side seam lines, and the two inseams, separately.

Can you even believe it? You just made your own pants pattern!

SEWING INSTRUCTIONS: Hem the pocket-opening edges, with a double-turned ¼" hem (or bias-tape facing), and press the center and bottom edges of the pockets under by ½". Lay the pockets on your front pant pieces, aligning the top and side seam edges, and pin. Edgestitch the two pressed-under edges, and baste the top and side-seam edges. Fold the underlap extensions in half lengthwise, right sides facing, and on each, stitch one of the short edges. Turn right-side out and press. Place one of the underlaps on the upper left-side seam of the back pant, with the open short end at the top, aligning raw edges, and stitch. Place the other on the upper left-side seam of the front pant, and stitch. With right sides facing, stitch pant

fronts to backs along inseams and side seams, leaving the left-side seam open at the underlaps. Finish the seams with an overedge zigzag or your preferred method. Fold the front underlap toward CF and edgestitch to front pant along the long side. With the back underlap extended out, underneath the front, stitch across the short bottom ends of both underlaps, from the outside of the pant. Now turn one leg right-side out, and stuff this leg inside the other (the one still wrong side out), matching up your front and back rise seams. Be sure the intersecting inseams meet, and stitch the rise seam. You may want to do a double-row of stitching, about ¹⁄₁₆" apart, for added security and finish the seam. Turn the pants right-side out. Seam the front outer waistband to the back, along the right-side seam, and press the seam open. Repeat for the waistband facings. Sew the outer waistband to the pant along the waist line, making sure the back waistband extension matches up to the underlap. Sew the waistband facing, right sides facing, to the waistband, along the top edge and the two short edges. Flip the facing to the inside, tuck the lower edge under, and press. Baste the waistband seam from the inside, then edgestitch from the outside, and remove the basting. Hem your pants, using a double-turned ½" hem. Complete them by making buttonholes in the front left waistband, and along the front left-side seam, and stitching buttons to the back waistband and underlap.

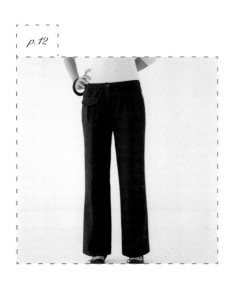

p.12

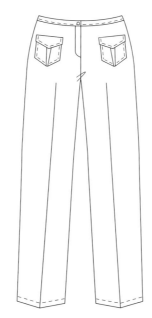

Pant Variation 1: ANNIE TROUSERS

To make these fancy grown-up trousers, we're just going to widen the leg of the Basic Pant from page 104 and add pleated flap pockets. No one will ever guess you made these yourself! Whip up a pair in a wool gabardine or suiting fabric to really do them justice. You'll need two big pieces of paper, big enough to trace your Basic Pant patterns from page 104 onto, plus some scraps.

1. WIDEN THE LEG

Trace your front pant pattern from the Basic Pant (page 106) onto a new sheet of paper. Add 1" to each side of leg at cuff, and blend to original seam lines at crotch and hip. Add SA.

2. ADD FRONT FLY EXTENSION

Extend the waist line out 2" from CF. Square a line down from this point, parallel to CF, for about 5" or desired fly length. The fly extension should end above where the rise seam begins to curve. Connect the fly line over to the rise seam with a perpendicular line. Notch the top edge of pattern at CF, and 1" to the right, indicating where the extension will fold back. Also notch the bottom edge of the fly extension at the 1" fold (see diagram).

Repeat the leg-widening step for the back pant.

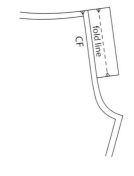

step 2

3. MAKE THE POCKET

On a small piece of paper, draft a rectangle the length and width you want your pocket to be. Add an extra 2" to the width for the box pleat. To make the **pleat**, draw a vertical line down the center of the pocket, and draw two more parallel lines on either side of the center line, each ½" apart. If you want to make this a pointed pocket, angle the corners beginning from the outer two pleat lines (the line between the pleat lines will remain straight). Add SA to all sides. Extend and notch all five pleat lines, at the top and bottom of pocket, to indicate where the pleat will be folded. Fold the pleat before you cut out the pocket, to shape the lower edge.

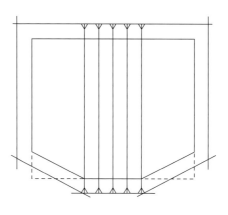

step 3

4. MAKE THE POCKET FLAP

On another scrap of paper, draft a rectangle the width of your *finished* pocket (excluding pleat) plus ¼", by the desired length of your flap. Angle the corners if you want (be sure to use the same angle as you did on the pocket). Add SA to all sides of the flap.

5. MAKE THE WAISTBAND

You'll need to alter the waistband from the Basic Pant for the front zipper opening. Trace the folded front waistband piece onto a new piece of paper. Add SA to CF (this piece won't be cut on the fold for this style). Label this piece "left front waistband." Trace the original folded front waistband again, this time adding a 1½" extension to CF (1" extension + SA). Label this piece "right front waistband." Trace the back waistband, and remove the extension.

6. LABEL AND TRUE YOUR PATTERN PIECES

Label your pattern pieces with CF and/or CB, grain line, your style name, the name of each pattern piece (front and back pant, left and right front waistband, back waistband, pocket, and flap), size or key measurements, and cutting instructions (front and back pant pieces are "cut 2," left and right front waistband, back waistband, and pocket are all "cut 2," and the pocket flap is "cut 4"). Check that all corresponding pieces match along seam lines.

SEWING INSTRUCTIONS: Fold the pocket pleats at notches, press, and edgestitch, if desired. Hem the top edge of the pocket (with the pleat folded) with a double-turned ¼" hem. Press the side and bottom SAs under and pin to the pant. Edgestitch the pocket to the pant. With right sides facing, stitch around the sides and lower edges of pocket flap. Turn right-side out, press, and edgestitch. Finish the raw edges together with an overedge zigzag. Lay the flap above the pocket, right-side down and raw edge toward pocket top. Stitch the flap to the pant, ½" from the raw edge. Flip down and topstitch ¼" from the top edge. Repeat for the other side. With right sides facing, seam pant fronts to backs along the inseams and side seams, and finish with an overedge zigzag. On the right leg, fold the fly extension back at the notches, and fold again on CF. Baste the fly along the inner edge. On the left leg, finish the edge of the fly extension with an overedge zigzag. Fold the fly back at the first set of notches, but not CF, so it extends out from CF. Baste. Stitch the zipper into fly. Sew the rise seam, from the bottom of the zipper extension to the back waist, and finish the seam edges. Seam the front outer waistband pieces to the back, along both side seams, and press the seams open. Repeat for the waistband facings. Sew the outer waistband to the skirt along the waist line, making sure the left front waistband extension matches up to the fly extension. Sew the waistband facing, right sides facing, to the waistband, along the top edge and the two short edges. Flip the facing to the inside, tuck the lower edge under, and press. Baste the waistband seam from the inside, then edgestitch from the outside, and remove the basting. Hem the trouser with a **blind hem** stitch for a polished look. Stitch buttonholes and a button at the CF waistband.

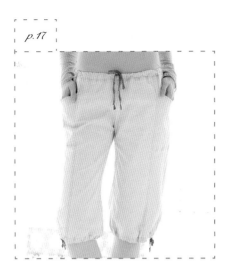

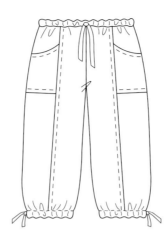

Pant Variation 2: OLIVIA KNICKERS

Adding a little extra room into your Basic Pant pattern makes for a casual, drawstring style perfect for yoga, errands, or just kicking around the house. We'll also add some fun wraparound pockets and ties at the knees. Try these in something soft and comfy, like cotton ripstop, washed silk twill, or gauze. You can use a shorter piece of paper for this style, a few inches longer than you want your pants but wide enough to fit both your front and back Basic Pant patterns.

1. ADD CENTER SEAMS AND FULLNESS, AND ELIMINATE THE SIDE SEAM

Trace your front pant pattern from the Basic Pant (page 105) onto the right side of the new paper, transferring the center grain line and crotch line. Shorten the pattern to your desired length, plus 1¼" for the drawstring casings. Lay your back pattern next to the front, overlapping the side seams at the hip and lining up at the crotch lines, and trace, including the center grain line. Extend the waist line across the gap where the side seam was, blending it into a smooth continuous line. Draw new seam lines, 1½" over from the original grain lines, toward each other. Cut the patterns apart on both of these new lines. Tape on a 1½" extension (1" + ½" SA) to each side of the 4 cut edges.

2. MAKE THE WAISTBAND CASING

This waistband can be a simple rectangle. Measure across the top waist line edges of all three (front, side, and back) pattern pieces, excluding the SA. Add them together and add another ½" for SA. Draft a rectangle this long, by 3" wide (1" doubled, + ½" SA on each side). Label one of the short sides "CB on fold."

3. MAKE THE POCKET

Draw on your side pant piece the shape and placement of your wraparound pocket, which will extend all the way from the front center seam to the back center seam. The top edge of the pocket should curve downward in the middle. Transfer this shape to a scrap of paper, using a pushpin or carbon paper. Add SA to all sides of the pocket. Notch the side pant pattern where the pocket will be placed.

4. LABEL AND TRUE YOUR PATTERN PIECES

Label your pattern pieces with CF and/or CB, grain line, your style name, the name of each pattern piece (front, side, and back pant, waistband casing, and pocket), size or key measurements, and cutting instructions (front, side, and back pant are all "cut 2," waistband casing is "cut 1 on fold," and pocket is "cut 2"). Check that all corresponding pieces match up along seam lines.

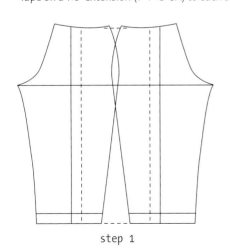

step 1

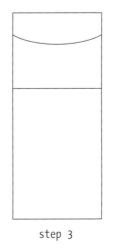

step 3

SEWING INSTRUCTIONS: Hem the top edge of the pocket with a double-turned ¼" hem. Press under SA on the bottom edge of the pocket only. Place the pocket on your side pant piece, as indicated by the notches, and edgestitch the bottom edge of pocket to the pant. Baste along both side edges of the pocket. Seam the front, side, and back pant pieces together, using flat-felled seams. Stitch the rise seam and finish with an overedge zigzag. For the drawstrings, make two buttonholes, 1" apart, 1½" up from bottom edge at center of each side pant piece. Make buttonholes 1" from each short end of the waistband casing, and ¾" up from the long edge (see diagram). Seam the waistband along the short end, fold it in half lengthwise, and seam to the waist of pants, placing the seam at CF. Finish the seam with an overedge zigzag or bias binding. Hem the pants with a ½" turn, then a ¾" turn, and edgestitch. Lace your choice of drawstring (cord, twill tape, or self-fabric drawstrings) through the waist and knee casings.

Part 3

CUSTOMIZING, FITTING, AND GRADING

Stylizing

Thus far I have given you detailed instructions on how
to execute patterns for garments that I've designed.
I am a firm believer that the best way to learn is by
doing, so hopefully you've been making the projects and
absorbing the concepts as you've been going along. But
I won't be able to sleep peacefully at night until I
believe that you, dear reader, are busy dreaming and
drafting up your own concoctions!

At this point, you are developing quite a library of
basic patterns. And if you've been making the variations
as well, you can see how, by tweaking the basics, your
options grow exponentially. A few more techniques
can help you get even more style mileage out of your
patterns. We have touched on some of these already in
many of the projects, but I would like to expand on each
one individually, so that you can fully understand the
principles and apply them to your own designs.

The techniques include adding flare or fullness through
the slash-and-spread method, and adding interior seams
and details, like yokes or pockets.

Slash and Spread

I know the name sounds scary, like something you hope never happens to you in a dark alley, and believe me, I've tried to come up with something better! (For the record, I didn't make it up; it's exactly what the technique was called when I learned it in fashion design school back in the '80s—gulp, did I just admit that?) However, once you see what **slash and spread** means, you'll see that the name fits perfectly, since it's literally what you do.

OK, let me explain the idea, and then we'll put it into action. Remember how we added some extra fullness in the Charlotte Top (page 69) by adding a 1" extension onto CF and CB? And then how we sliced open the sleeve and added a wedge of space in there? These are both simplified examples of slashing and spreading. Only tiny amounts of fullness were added in these situations, and both of them were to be gathered up in the final result. But this is also how we add the kind of flare that makes a skirt twirly or a sleeve belled. You may also recall how, in our very first project, the Basic Skirt (page 40), I said that you shouldn't add more than a few inches of flare at that time, because "more flare than that needs to be added in a way that we'll learn later." Well, guess what? It's later!

See, if you drafted a skirt the way I explained in that chapter and tried to make a huge sweep, you would end up with two droopy flaps hanging by your ankles instead of a swirly, twirlable skirt. This is because all the fullness would have been added to the sides instead of being evenly distributed around the full circumference of the skirt. If, on the other hand, you sliced the skirt pattern into three to five even sections and spread them apart equally, you would be distributing the fullness throughout the skirt as you want. It's all about translating the two dimensions of a flat pattern into the three dimensions of a finished garment wrapping around a body. It will come more easily to some than others, but hang in there!

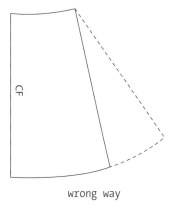

wrong way

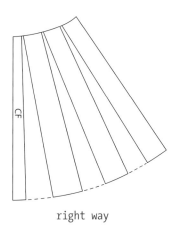

right way

p. 9

Phoebe Skirt

Let's try out the slashing and spreading technique in a little flared skating skirt with inset pockets. I made mine in a cross-dyed linen blend, but any crisp woven will work. For this project, you'll need your Basic Skirt pattern (page 40), two pieces of paper the same size, and two pieces of paper about twice as wide as the skirt pattern, plus some scraps.

1. Make a copy

Trace a copy of your front skirt pattern from the Basic Skirt (page 42) onto one of the same-sized pieces of paper, and cut it out. This way you won't have to slash your original master pattern. This is also a good time to adjust the length if you want your new skirt shorter or longer than the original. Include your SA, so you won't need to add it later.

2. Divide into sections

Depending on how much flare you want to add, you'll need to draw three to five lines down the length of your pattern, dividing it into four to six sections. For our purposes, we'll go with four, but know that if you're going for extreme twirlitude, you might want to go for the six. First, tape your dart closed (darts probably won't be necessary for this skirt, but if you find you need them, you can always add them back later). Then, use the right-side notch of your dart as the (approximate) center point, and make a mark here. Divide each of those two sections in half and mark. Do the same at the hemline, and connect the corresponding marks top to bottom, dividing the skirt into four sections. Now, starting from the bottom, cut on each line, until you are about ¼" from the waist SA line, and stop. This concludes the "slash" section of our project.

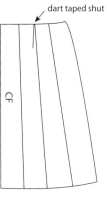

dart taped shut

CF

steps 1–2

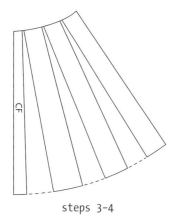

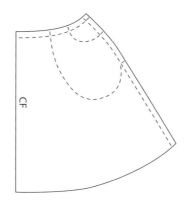

pocket lining   pocket facing

steps 3–4   step 6

3. ADD THE FLARE

Lay your slashed pattern onto one of your big pieces of paper, with CF aligned over the left-side edge of the paper. Keeping the CF waist point touching the left edge (CF) of the new pattern, open up the cuts and spread them out as much as you desire. The only rule is to make sure that you keep the sections relatively even (although the CF section should only be half the size of the others, since it's on the fold). You will notice that the shape of the waist line is changing completely, curving upward as you spread. This may seem weird, but I assure you it's normal, necessary even. When you're satisfied with the amount of flare you've added, tape, weight, or pushpin the pieces down to hold them still while you trace around the waist, side seam, and hem (don't trace the cut lines). This concludes the "spread" portion of our show!

4. CONNECT AND SMOOTH THE CURVES

Now we just need to clean up the curves. At the waist line, smooth the points out so you have a nice, even curve. At the hem line, con-

nect the gaps into a smooth curve as well. You may have to shave off some bits and add onto others in order to blend everything into one continuous line.

5. MAKE THE BACK AND CUT OUT

Repeat steps 1–4 to make the back skirt pattern, and cut out both patterns.

6. MAKE THE POCKET

On your front skirt, draw in your side and waist seam lines (you probably only have the SA lines), then sketch the shape you would like for your pocket opening (the part that will show on the skirt). It should begin on the waist line and end on the side seam. Be sure that your hand will fit through it! Now draw the shape of the inside pocket lining, which will not show from the outside. Using a pin or carbon paper, transfer two shapes onto new scraps of paper (see diagram): One will be the pocket lining (bordered by the pocket opening, waistline, inside pocket, and side seam), and the other will be the pocket facing (bordered by the waistline, side seam, and inside pocket). Add SA to all sides of

these two pattern pieces. Add SA to the pocket opening seam line on the skirt, and cut on this line.

7. MAKE THE WAISTBAND

A skirt with this much flare usually sits higher on the waist, so the straight waistband method should work fine, but you can make a shaped waistband if you prefer. Follow the instructions for either method in the skirt chapter.

8. LABEL AND TRUE YOUR PATTERN PIECES

Label your pattern pieces with CF and/or CB, grain line, your style name, the name of each pattern piece (front and back skirt, waistband, pocket facing, and pocket lining), size or key measurements, and cutting instructions (front and back skirt pieces are "cut 1 on fold," waistband [if straight] is "cut 1," and pocket lining and facing are "cut 2"). Notch CF, CB, and side seams on waistband piece. Notch CF and CB on waist line of skirt pieces. Check that front and back pieces match along side seam lines.

Sewing instructions: With right sides together, stitch the pocket linings to the skirt along the pocket opening curve. Flip the linings to the inside, and edgestitch the seam, if desired. With right sides together, sew the pocket facings to the linings along the curved pocket edge, and finish the seam with an overedge zigzag. Baste the three layers together along the waist and side-seam edges. Now seam the right-side seam of the skirt with a French seam, insert an invisible zipper in the left-side seam, and then stitch the remaining part of the seam and finish with a mock-French seam. Apply the waistband, button, and buttonhole as for the Rosie Skirt (page 49), and hem with a double-turned ½" hem.

p.19

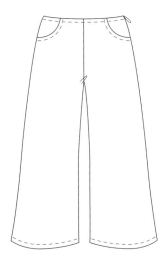

Carla Palazzo

You can use the exact same process from the Phoebe Skirt (page 119) with your Basic Pant pattern (page 104) to make a fuller pant leg, culotte, or skort. A wider pant tends to be more flattering to those of us with hips, so I've always been a fan of the style. My linen gingham gave these a nice flare, but a drapier woven would lend a softer look. You'll need your Basic Pant pattern, two pieces of paper the same size as your pattern pieces, and two much wider pieces, plus the usual scraps.

1. Make a copy
Trace copies of both your front and back pant patterns from the Basic Pant pattern (page 106).

2. Divide into sections
Divide each pattern piece into four sections, and draw the vertical slash lines from waist to hem. Cut, leaving them connected at the waist.

3. Add the flare
Spread the sections apart until the desired amount of flare is added (I spread mine about 1½" at each cut), and trace.

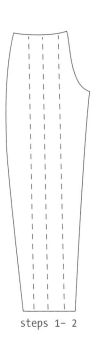
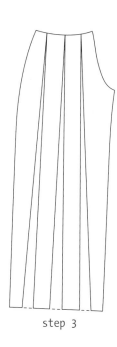

steps 1– 2   step 3

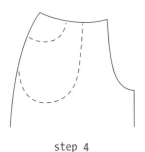

step 4

4. MAKE THE POCKET

On your front pant, sketch the shape you would like for your pocket opening (the part that will show). It should begin on the waist line and end on the side seam. Now draw the shape of the inside pocket lining, which will not show from the outside. Using a pin or carbon paper, transfer the two shapes onto new scraps of paper.

5. LABEL AND TRUE YOUR PATTERN PIECES

Label your pattern pieces with CF and/or CB, grain line, your style name, the name of each pattern piece (front and back pant, pocket facing, and pocket lining), size or key measurements, and cutting instructions (front and back pant pieces are "cut 2," and pocket lining and facing are "cut 2"). Check that front and back pieces match along side seam lines.

SEWING INSTRUCTIONS: With right sides together, stitch the pocket linings to the pant along the pocket opening curve. Flip the linings to the inside, and edgestitch the seam, if desired. With right sides together, sew the pocket facings to the linings along the curved pocket edge, and finish the seam with an overedge zigzag. Baste the three layers together along the waist and side seam edges. With right sides facing, stitch pant fronts to backs along inseams and side seams (finishing as you like), leaving the left-side seam open. Insert an invisible zipper at the upper left-side seam, then seam and finish the lower part of the seam with a mock-French seam. Now turn one leg right-side out, and stuff this leg inside the other (the one still wrong side out), matching up your front and back rise seams. Be sure the intersecting inseams meet, and stitch the rise seam from front waist to back. You may want to do a double row of stitching, about $1/16$" apart, and finish the seam. Turn the pants right-side out. Finish the waist with a bias-tape facing (see Insider Sewing Techniques, page 148, for complete instructions). Hem your pants, using a double-turned $1/2$" hem.

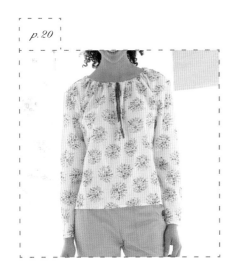

p. 20

MIHO SHIRT

Now let's try out the technique in a different situation, like, say, around a neckline, to be gathered up with a drawstring. We did this before in a small way for the Charlotte Top (page 69), but this time we'll really add a good amount of fullness all the way around the neckline. I used a vintage printed voile for this one; keep your fabric lightweight so the gathering won't be too bulky. For this one you'll need your Basic Shirt pattern (page 76), three sheets of paper the same size as your main pattern pieces (front, back, and sleeve), and two bigger pieces.

1. MAKE THE FRONT SHIRT

Start by tracing your front shirt pattern from the Basic Shirt (page 78) onto a same-size piece of paper. We won't be using the front placket for this shirt (it'll be cut on the fold at CF) but we'll leave the extra placket width in so the shirt will fit a little wider at the bottom (you can trim all or part of the placket off, if you don't want this extra room, but remember that this is a pullover shirt so it'll need a little space to get it on). Label the left-side placket edge as CF. Lower and widen the neckline as you like, and fix the neckline curve to be a 90°

angle at CF. Adjust the length of the shirt now, if you want to, as well (mine is 23"). This is the template of your new pattern; we'll just have to explode it to get the neck shirring!

2. SLASH AND SPREAD

Divide the neckline into six even sections (divide in half, then each half into thirds) and mark. From each of these points, draw a line, perpendicular to the neckline curve, radiating out until it meets either the armhole, the side seam, or the hem line. Cut on each of these lines, starting at the neck, and leave the last ¼" uncut. Now lay this unwieldy thing onto one of your larger sheets of paper, aligning CF with the paper's left edge. Spread your slashes apart evenly; anywhere from ½" to 1" (each) should be enough, depending how much you want your neckline to gather. When you are satisfied, tape or weight the pieces down, and trace around all outer edges. Remove the slashed pattern, and connect the spaces at the neckline, smoothing it into one continuous curve. Smooth out the armhole, side seam, and hemlines as well, eliminating any points. Check that all your corners are still right angles.

3. MAKE THE BACK SHIRT

Repeat steps 1 and 2 for the back. You may want to add an extension to CB to allow extra fullness at the bottom (as you did with the front

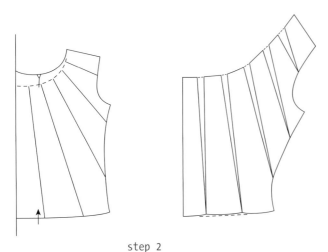

step 2

How Much to Spread?

Gathering is a very useful, and decorative, technique that you can use in lots of ways. It can be adjustable, as with a drawstring casing, or permanently set into place by a seam. Essentially, it is fitting a larger piece of fabric into a smaller piece. When gathering is very slight, it's called *shirring*. To figure out how far apart to spread your slashed openings, measure the length of the seam you'll be gathering the enlarged piece into. Then decide what "gathering ratio" you want to use. A ratio of 1.25:1 is light shirring; 1.5:1 is medium shirring; 2:1 is kind of your standard gathering; and 3:1 is pretty extreme gathering (picture the waist of a '50s prom dress and you'll get the idea!). If you're having trouble

visualizing this, try some swatches of different gathering ratios to decide what will work best for the project you're working on.

So let's say you've decided a 1.5:1 ratio will be ideal, and the seam you'll be gathering it into measures 9". That means you'll want your enlarged seam line to be 13.5" long (9" x 1.5). So if you are making three slashes, and you need to add 4.5" of gathering, you'll spread each one out by 1.5" (4.5" divided by 3). If all this math gives you a headache, you can also just wing it, but be prepared for mixed results!

---

by keeping the placket extension). You can do fewer slashes for the back neck, since it is much smaller than the front; probably three are enough.

4. MARK THE SLITS

Notch the lower front and back side seams, 2" up from hem line, to indicate slits.

5. MAKE THE SLEEVE

Trace a copy of your sleeve pattern from the Basic Shirt (page 81) onto a new sheet of paper. Divide into thirds vertically, and slash from the bottom, leaving the top ¼" connected. Slash and spread about ½" to ¾" to add a little flare to the sleeve. Clean up the cuff line and smooth the cap. Add notches to indicate slits at the cuff, along the underarm seam.

6. MAKE THE NECK CASING

Measure the length of your combined front and back necklines, and add 1" SA. Draw a rectangle this long, by 2" wide (¾" casing x 2 + ½" total SA).

7. LABEL AND TRUE YOUR PATTERN PIECES

Label your pattern pieces with CF and/or CB, grain line, your style name, the name of each pattern piece (front and back shirt, sleeve, and neck casing), size or key measurements, and cutting instructions (front and back shirt are "cut 1 on fold," sleeve is "cut 2," and neck casing is "cut 1"). Notch shoulder seams, CF and CB on neck casing, and CF/CB on shirt pieces. Check that all corresponding pieces match along seam lines.

SEWING INSTRUCTIONS: Sew front to back along side seams (above notches) and shoulder seams, and finish edges. Make buttonholes 1" apart at CF of neck casing piece (fold band in half lengthwise to determine the correct placement from neck edge), seam the short ends of the casing, fold wrong sides together and sew it to the neckline. Sew the underarm seams of sleeves (above notches), finish, and set the sleeves into your armholes. Hem the cuffs and bottom hem with a double-turned ½" hem, and stitch around slits at ¼".

SOFIE T

Isn't it great being a designer? You'll never need to buy another pattern again! Another helpful trick to have in your toolbox is a knack for making interior seams, such as the little placket in this adorable blouse. Mine is in a lusciously soft fine cotton jersey; any light- to medium-weight T-shirt knit will suit this style. This sweet little top will be based on your Basic T pattern (page 76). You'll need three pieces of paper the same size as the originals (front, back and sleeve) and three a little bigger.

1. MAKE THE FRONT SHIRT

Trace a copy of your front shirt pattern from the Basic T (page 78) onto fresh paper. Adjust the neckline shape if you want to; you may want to make it a bit lower and wider for this style, but it's your call (I made mine about an inch lower and wider than my Basic T neckline). Then draw the placket, as you'd like it. Cut the placket out, and set it aside. On the shirt piece, draw four or five slash lines radiating out from the placket seam. Where you place the lines determines where you will add shirring, so if you only want it on the bottom edge of the placket, only slash there, but if you want it all around, slash accordingly. Make at least two of your lines extend down to the hemline, as we can add some flare there to make this a swingier top. Now cut on the slash lines, starting from the placket, and leaving ¼" uncut on lines ending at the armhole or side seam, but cutting all the way through the ones that end on the hem. Spread apart the slashes around the placket area, being careful not to add too much shirring here. A 1.25:1 ratio is good for slight shirring. Spread the slashes at the hemline an inch or so each. Tape or weight everything down, trace around the outer edges, and clean it all up as in step 4 of the Phoebe Skirt (page 120). Now add SA to the placket seam and the outer edge of your placket piece.

step 1

Stylizing ⊬ 129

2. MAKE THE BACK SHIRT

For the back of this style, let's just add a little flare to the hem so it matches the front. Draw two or three vertical slash lines from the neck seam to hem. Cut, leaving ¼" attached at the neck, and spread 1" (or whatever you did for the front) at the hem. Trace and clean up the curves. Draw a slight cutaway curve at the top of CB for a keyhole, and cut it out.

3. MAKE THE SLEEVE

Use your new skills to slash and spread some fullness into the bottom of your sleeve, to be gathered up with a binding.

4. LABEL AND TRUE YOUR PATTERN PIECES

Label your pattern pieces with CF and/or CB, grain line, your style name, the name of each pattern piece (front and back shirt, placket, and sleeve), size or key measurements, and cutting instructions (front and back shirt are "cut 1 on fold," placket is "cut 2 on fold," and sleeve is "cut 2"). Add a note on the front piece to cut approximately 2 yards of 1½" self-fabric strips to use as bindings at neck, keyhole, and cuffs. Notch CF on front and yoke pieces. Check that all corresponding pieces match along seam lines.

SEWING INSTRUCTIONS: On the shirt front piece, run two rows of gathering stitches around the placket seam. Gather to fit the placket and sew them together. Press under the outer edge of the placket facing piece, and baste to the inside of placket. Edgestitch the placket from the right side. Sew the front to back at the shoulder and side seams. Finish the back keyhole edge with a ⅜" self-binding. Finish the neckline with the same binding, extending into long ties at CB. Sew the underarm seams of sleeves and set into armholes. Gather the cuffs as desired, and bind as with the neck. Hem the top with a double-turned ½" hem. Sew some tiny buttons onto the placket, if desired.

p. 16

Kathy Dress

This little chemise requires curving the yoke seam and opening up the neckline to gather into the yoke. We'll also add some built-in pockets. Try it in almost any woven fabric that you love; I used a nice, heavy cotton ticking stripe. It's based on your Miette Dress pattern (page 98), and borrows the sleeves from the Miho Shirt (page 126), only we'll gather them up at the cuff. You'll need four large sheets of paper, big enough to accommodate the Miette pattern, plus a little extra.

1. Make the front dress and yoke

Trace the Miette front pattern (page 98) onto a new piece of paper. Use the original side-seam line with waist shaping, not the straightened one. Alter the neckline as you like before drafting the yoke (I kept mine the same). Along the neckline, measure out 2" (or your desired yoke width) all around, to establish the yoke seam. Cut the pattern out, and cut it apart on the yoke seam line. On the front-body piece, draw four slash lines radiating out from the neckline, as you did for the Miho Shirt. Cut on the lines, starting from the yoke, and leaving them connected at the other ends. Spread each slash about an inch apart and trace around the outer pattern edges. Connect the gaps, smooth the curves, and add SA to the yoke seam line. Add SA to the same seam on the yoke pattern piece as well.

2. Make the back dress

Repeat step 1, this time using the Miette back pattern, to make the back dress and yoke.

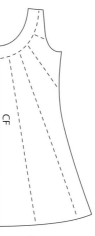

step 1

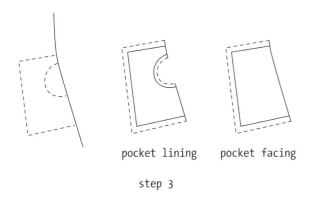

pocket lining   pocket facing

step 3

3. MAKE THE POCKET

On your front dress, draw in the shape you would like for your pocket opening. It should be a semicircle that begins and ends on the side seam. Now draw the shape of the inside pocket lining, which will not show from the outside. Using a pin or carbon paper, transfer the two shapes onto new scraps of paper (see diagram): One will be the pocket lining (bordered by the pocket opening, three sides of the inside pocket, and side seam), and the other will be the pocket facing (bordered by the side seam and the three sides of the inside pocket). Add SA to all sides of these two pattern pieces. Add SA to the pocket opening seam line on the dress, and cut on this line.

4. MAKE THE CUFF BINDING

You will use the sleeve from the Miho Shirt (page 128), but for this dress we're going to gather it into a ½" self binding. To make the pattern piece, draw a rectangle 2" (that's ½" x 4) by a comfortable length around your wrist,

plus 1" SA. The smaller you make the binding, the more gathered your cuff will be. Just be sure to make it big enough for your hand to fit through!

5. LABEL AND TRUE YOUR PATTERN PIECES

Label your pattern pieces with CF and/or CB, grain line, your style name, the name of each pattern piece (front and back dress, front and back yoke, sleeve [either make a copy of the Miho sleeve, or put a note on the front piece to borrow it], and cuff binding), size or key measurements, and cutting instructions (front and back dress are "cut 1 on fold," yokes are "cut 2 on fold," and cuff binding is "cut 2"). Notch CF/CB on front, back, and yoke pieces. Check that all corresponding pieces match along seam lines.

SEWING INSTRUCTIONS: With right sides together, stitch the pocket linings to the dress front along the pocket openings. Flip to the inside, press, and edgestitch the pocket opening seam. Then sew the pocket facings to the pocket linings, and finish the seam edges with an overedge zigzag. Topstitch around the pocket lining, from the right side of the dress. Seam the front to back along the shoulder and side seams, and finish. Sew the front yokes to the back yokes at the shoulders (one pair will be facings). Gather the neckline and pin to the yoke, matching shoulder seams and CF/CB. Seam the yoke to the dress, then sew the yoke facing to the yoke at the neckline. Flip the facing to the inside, and turn under the seam allowance along the yoke seam. Baste the facing along the yoke seam from the inside, then edgestitch it from the right side, and remove the basting. Set in the sleeves and gather and bind the cuff edges. Hem the dress with a ½" double-turned hem.

Throw a Fit

OK, so you've made your first pattern! Let's say it's your A-line skirt. Now it's time to cut it out of that adorable vintage Holly Hobbie fabric you scored at the flea market in Ohio ten years ago, and have been saving for just the *perfect* project, right? Wrongo. I know you're excited (after all, this is the moment you've been waiting for!), but before you cut a newly made pattern out of your "real" (i.e., expensive or irreplaceable) fabric, you should always make a muslin to test out the fit and silhouette. It really doesn't take long, and you'll save yourself a whole lot of heartache.

What Is Muslin, Exactly?

First, let me say a few words about the term *muslin*. As I mentioned earlier, there are two general uses for the term, and a few contributing factors that can lead to all kinds of confusion. Let's start with the meaning I referenced a moment ago when I said "you should always make a muslin." A muslin is a prototype, a draft, a test sample. We make one to see how a pattern looks and fits on a three-dimensional form. Because we draft our patterns flat, in only two dimensions, and out of paper, which doesn't hang or drape the way fabric does, it's not until we cut the pattern in cloth, stitch the seams and put it on, that we really have a clue how it looks.

The second meaning of *muslin* is the fabric that prototypes are traditionally made from: unbleached, plain-weave, lightweight, inexpensive cotton. Muslin, the fabric, works fine as the test fabric for certain samples, but honestly, I rarely use it. Why? Well, I have my reasons:

The first is that your test fabric should be a reasonable stand-in for your "real" fabric. So, if it's a T-shirt pattern, you should test it in a knit. If it's a stretch-woven pant, test it in a stretch-woven. If it's going to be a silk chiffon gown, you might make the sample in poly chiffon. And a winter coat prototype should be made up in something thick and coatlike to give the most accurate estimation. Only if your final fabric will have the same properties as muslin should you consider using it for your test garment.

The second is that muslin isn't attractive. I know, I know, looks aren't everything. But they never hurt, right? My point is, when you come across a sale bin of $1-a-yard remnants, or find a pretty sheet at the thrift store, snatch these goodies up to use as "muslin." Then, if it turns out your pattern *is* right-on, you've got a garment! Which brings me to my third reason for not using the stuff: It's not always cheap. Actual, official muslin often costs $5 a yard or more, so keep an eye out for cuter, bargain-priced alternatives and keep a supply of options on hand. Still, whatever fabric you are using for your samples will commonly be referred to as *muslin*, even if it's really hot-pink jersey from a recycled T-shirt.

So, getting back to the confusing part, let me try to be clear. Your muslin, the prototype, may, or may not, be made from muslin, the fabric. And your muslin, the fabric, may or may not be actual muslin at all. Any questions?

Making the Muslin

Let's move on to actually making the muslin. The basic idea is to cut it out from your pattern (transferring any markings), and stitch it together as you would the final garment. However, there are a few key differences.

For starters, you'll want to stitch your muslin seams using a basting stitch. This just means you'll set your machine to the longest stitch length, usually four millimeters. The reason to baste your seams for the muslin is that basting is easy to rip out, and since we are in the testing stage, there is a chance that you will need to rip all or part of a seam or dart open, in order to move it or let it out a bit. Baste all the major seams, leaving open any areas where a zipper or other closure will be inserted. Also baste darts, tucks, and anything else necessary to accurately show the fit of the pattern.

You can leave all of your edges unfinished (in other words, don't sew any hems, facings, or other finishing devices), and definitely don't bother finishing your seam allowance edges or sewing French seams at this point. Don't add pockets, belt loops, or any other decorative features. A muslin is temporary, so no unnecessary work should be done, unless it's important to you for some reason. If, say, you are making your ultimate pair of Dream Pants and want to work out the perfect length, so you can cut out ten pairs and know they'll all be just right, go for it and stitch those hems. Or if your entire dress design hinges on the oversized flowerpot-shaped pockets, by all means mock them up! But otherwise you can just leave the finishing for the real thing.

Other, more functional details can be tested in a low-commitment way. For example, you might just fold your waistband and baste it on in one step, rather than doing the more complicated multistep

method you'll use for the real thing. We just need to see how the pattern shapes work together and fit on your body for now. It's a good idea to stay-stitch any unfinished curves that might get pulled or stretched in the trying-on process, such as the waist or neckline. Stay-stitching will prevent these curves from getting stretched out and changing the fit.

OK, let's get back to your skirt muslin. You've basted your darts and seams, kept open the left hip side seam where the zipper will go (so you can get the skirt on), and stay-stitched the waist. I'd also recommend a good pressing at this point, to flatten your darts and seams and make it look crisp and new. What to do now? Try it on, of course!

The Fitting

You'll want a full-length mirror nearby, and some safety pins, straight pins, and a marking device handy (I like those blue disappearing-ink pens). Put the skirt on, and use some safety pins to close up the zipper opening (try to do it accurately, on the actual seam line). I prefer safety pins for this because they won't fall out or poke you. Now, step back and take a look. I'll bet it looks smashing! Remember, we're only analyzing for fit and overall silhouette; you may need to use a little visualization to see the final picture.

Here are some things to think about as you assess your handiwork:

Does the size seem right? Is there enough room to breathe, and can you walk, sit, and bend down to tie your shoes? Do you like where the waistline sits, or is it too high or too low? (Remember that you'll lose the ½" of SA when it's finished.) How's the length? (Again, you'll lose a full inch when you hem it, so pin it up if you want to see the finished length.) Are you satisfied with the amount of flare and the silhouette? Are the darts nipping in at the right places? Do they need to pinch out more or less fullness, to make the waistline lie flat against your body? You may find you don't need the front darts at all, as some of us (ahem) protrude out at the front waist more than we nip in. I'm just saying . . .

This is a good time to determine or confirm the placement of decorative elements like pockets, appliqués, or stylized seams. Mock up pockets by cutting them out, sans SA, and pinning them on.

If you feel like you do want to make some tweaks, I find it easiest to take the muslin off and put it back on *inside out*. This way you have easy access to all of the "inner workings," and you can pinch and pin without having to flip it later. If you needed to rip any seams (using your seam ripper, not your hands), do so before you put it back on. Once you've got the skirt on inside out, pin and mark wherever you see corrections you'll want to make on the pattern. If you need more fabric anywhere (say, if you want to raise the waistline, add more flare, or give more room through the hips) just pin on a scrap of fabric to extend the muslin pattern piece. Sculpt your creation to fit just how you want it, as this is your golden opportunity, while you have it on your body. You see, as long as we're drafting flat, on paper laid on a table, we're really only making our best guess as to what will happen in the third dimension. The fitting is when we can finally begin to see how the flat pattern translates to the full-circumference, actual end result. Every time you make a muslin and fit it, you will gain all kinds of subtle understanding that will help you as you draft your next pattern.

When you're done fiddling with the muslin, make a mark with chalk or a disappearing marker, everywhere you pinned, in case any pins fall out. Carefully take it off. Check that you have marked all your corrections, and remove all pins, and basting stitches. The only pins to keep are the ones you may have used to graft on an extension. Lay your separated muslin pieces on top of your paper pattern, and transfer the marks to your pattern with dressmaker's carbon or a pushpin. Because you pinned and marked the muslin on your body, you will probably need to true up or smooth out any new lines, as they'll tend to be kind of wobbly. If your adjustments are major, you may want to make a second muslin, but most likely you just made subtle improvements and your pattern should be ready to proceed to the final.

And if you're happy with the way your muslin looks and fits, your pattern is already finished. *Now* you can break out the beloved Holly Hobbie fabric, and go to town!

Making the Grade

Suppose you've made yourself a sweet dress, and now your best friend wants one too. You'd love to make her one, but she's a size 6 and you're more like a 10. Or maybe you want to start selling your hot new skirts at craft fairs, but you realize you'll need to offer a range of sizes. What's a patternmaker to do? Well, my dear, you need to grade.

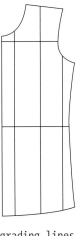

grading lines

Grading is the art of sizing patterns up or down from the original size at which they were drafted. Clothing manufacturers usually make their first samples at a size 6 or 8, and grade up and down from there. So you can imagine why a size 14 can be pretty distorted, if it started out being fit for someone much smaller. There are no industry standards for garment sizes or the grade (difference) between each size, which is why finding clothes that fit can be so frustrating.

If you want to grade a pattern to fit a specific person, take her measurements, and compare them to the original ones used in drafting the pattern (this is why I like to have the measurements written right on the pattern itself; then they're always right there when you need them). Find the differences between each pair of measurements (her waist to your waist, for instance) and divide that number by 4 (for horizontal dimensions only) to figure out how much you'll need to spread (or shrink) each part of a pattern piece. Chances are, you will be making an "uneven grade," because the difference between each set of measurements will vary.

Once you get the hang of patternmaking and you're ready to move on to the next step, you might want to consider creating a range of sizes to sell. To do this, you will make an "even grade." This means that the difference in bust size between your size Medium and Large (say, 2") will be the same as the difference in hip size. All the full-circumference (bust, waist, hip) horizontal measurements will increase by the same amount. The half-circumference measurements (neck width, shoulder width) will increase equally by a smaller amount. And the vertical measurements will increase proportionally at the same rate. How much difference you'll put between sizes will be up to you. You might want to do some research, either by collecting the measurements of as many members of your target market as you can or by studying the size charts in catalogs and Web sites of companies that appeal to the same market.

Whether you'll be making an even or uneven grade, the basic method will be the same. It's similar to the process of "slashing and spreading" explained on page 118. Let's take your Basic T front (page 60), and make a copy of it. You'll need to draw three vertical lines and two horizontal ones. The verticals will all be parallel to CF: one from the lower neckline to hem, one from shoulder seam to hem, and one from the lower armhole to hem. These lines will be where you add (or subtract) width to the pattern. The horizontals will both be perpendicular to CF: one from armhole to CF (it may or may not intersect the neckline), and one from the side seam to CF. These indicate where you'll add (or subtract) length. (See diagram above.) You should also remove the SA from your pattern, to be more accurate and minimize confusion. Cut on all five lines, and lay the pieces on a new sheet of paper. Now you can spread the pieces apart, or overlap them, until the pattern fits the desired new measurements. Tape or weight them down and trace around the outer edges, and smooth or fill in gaps and points. That wasn't so hard! Repeat the process for the remaining pattern pieces, and re-true your pattern when you're done, by checking that all corresponding seam lines match up. Good work; you deserve an A+!

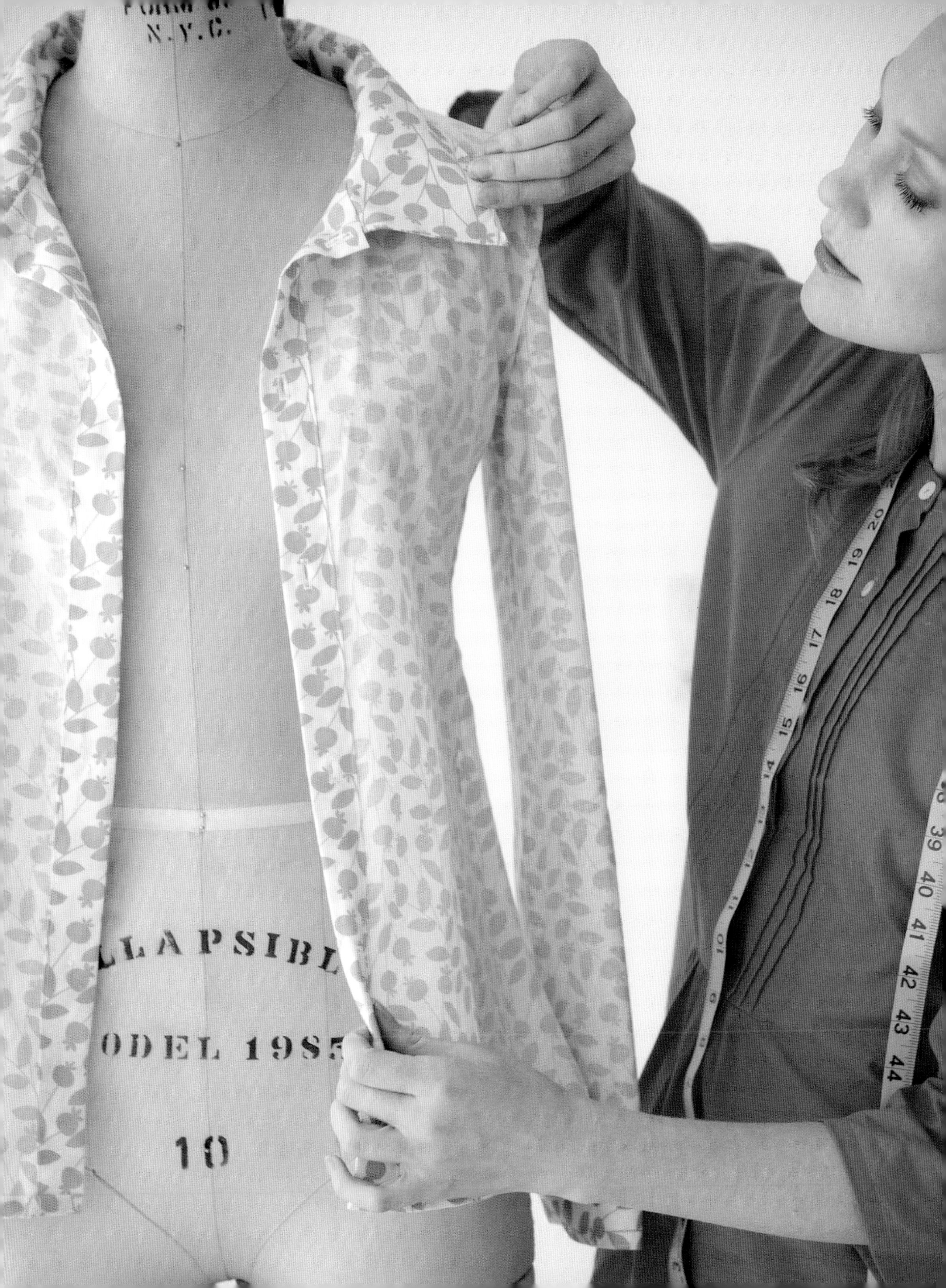
N.Y.C.
LLAPSIBL
ODEL 1985
10

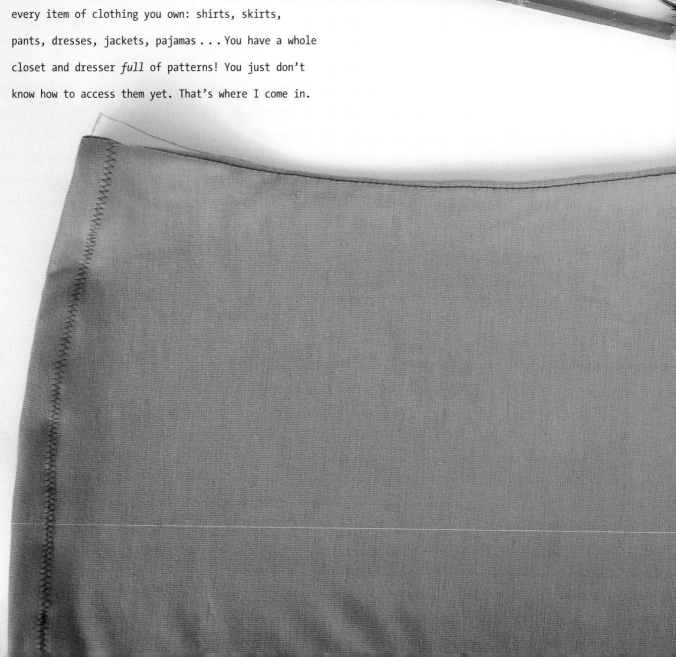

Making Patterns from Existing Clothes

What if I told you that, before you even picked up this book, you already owned a hundred or more patterns for clothes that fit you? I imagine you would say something along the lines of, "What on earth are you talking about? No I don't!"

But I am not joking—you really do! I mean, one hundred is just a rough guesstimate; you may have more, you may have less. What I'm referring to is every item of clothing you own: shirts, skirts, pants, dresses, jackets, pajamas . . . You have a whole closet and dresser *full* of patterns! You just don't know how to access them yet. That's where I come in.

Making patterns from scratch is obviously an invaluable skill, and you are going to love your new capabilities. But sometimes you don't have to start *completely* from scratch, with your tape measure and a blank sheet of paper. Sometimes, you will find that much of the work has already been done for you, so why reinvent the T-shirt? Think of your closet as an encyclopedia, a whole library of reference material right at your fingertips. Half the time, when you begin drafting a new pattern, you are probably picturing something in your closet already, anyway. So why not begin there?

Let's say you want to make yourself the most perfect T-shirt pattern, so that you can make yourself ten more just like that faded green one that you've worn to death. You could start from your own measurements, and draft a new pattern, and I've no doubt it would be one well-fitting T. However, it may not have the subtle nuances that make the faded green one your *favoritest T evah*. Because what you've never noticed about that one is how the shoulder seam is dropped just slightly toward the front. And how the bottom hem is just a little baggy, so it never rides up. And how the neckline is a little wider than normal, almost a boat neck. And how the sleeves are extra long, so they wrinkle at the wrist, and the bust is just a bit snug, so it hugs you just right. See what I mean? If you start by **rubbing off** a pattern from your actual shirt, you'll automatically have all that stuff built in. And no, contrary to morbid belief, you don't have to ruin the original to glean a pattern from it. So what exactly are we waiting for?

You'll Need:
One simple garment you'd like to rub off (for now, stick to something without darts, pleats, or gathering; a T-shirt or simple dress is ideal)

A few sheets of paper

Pushpins and/or a needle-point tracing wheel

Pencil and eraser

Ruler and curve

Cutting mat, cardboard, or a table you can pin into

You must think in reverse order, since you will be unearthing the original pattern shapes from a finished piece of clothing. The process is a bit like detective work. The key principle to keep in mind, as you trace the pattern off the garment, is that you will only focus on *one pattern piece at a time*. Start by identifying the front pattern piece on your garment.

Fold the front piece along CF, so that the shoulder seams, armholes, and side seams match up to their counterparts on the other side. The neckline and hemline should be folded in half, and these two halves should be matched up as well. You might find that the two sides of the garment don't seem to be identical, or are difficult to line up. This is because many fabrics (especially knits) torque, or twist, after they are washed, and as a result, your two halves may be very far out of alignment. Just do the best you can to get both layers to lie smoothly, and choose one side to be your pattern guide. Put this side on top, so that you can see it clearly.

Now lay the CF fold on the edge of your paper, and try to make the entire folded front of your garment lie flat on the paper. Be aware that any time you fold a part in half, as we're doing here, that fold *must* be a straight line (to be cut on the fold) on the pattern. If you have to force the fold to be a straight line, do so. You may need to pin sections in place with pushpins, to hold everything stable. Try to figure out exactly what the shape would have once been, when the front piece was originally cut out, before it was sewn to anything else. So if the neckband seems to be gathering up the neckline slightly (a clue would be puckering along the neckband), stretch it out a little and pin it in place.

When you have the front as stable and true to its original form as you can, go ahead and trace it. The shoulder seam, side seam and hemline are easy; just trace around them with your pencil. For the neckline and armhole, just use a pushpin or the needle-point tracing wheel if you have one, to transfer the seam line through to your paper with a series of pinholes. Be gentle; I might not do this with my best silk charmeuse blouse. But most cottons and knits should hold up fine.

Remove the garment, and fill in your pinhole lines with your pencil. Your lines and curves may be somewhat wobbly or awkward, so try to recreate their original clean, smooth shapes, based on your experience drafting your own patterns. Note that any intersecting seams are (or should be) 90°, as always. All that's left to do is add SA, and repeat the process for the other parts. If the back of the garment appears to be the same as the front, except for the neckline, make a copy of the front pattern piece and just rub off the back neckline. Always remember to make sure the piece you are tracing is flat, and any surrounding parts can be wrinkled and bunched any which way. For example, in order to get the sleeve to lie truly flat, and find the S-shape that forms the cap, you'll have to sort of bunch up the armhole and the rest of the body. Just take one piece at a time, and soon your pattern library will require the Dewey Decimal system to keep it organized!

Insider Sewing Techniques

At first, it may throw you that when you design and make your own patterns, they don't come with instruction manuals for how to sew them together. On the other hand, can you ever really understand what those instructions are saying? Deciphering them can be the hardest part of sewing from commercial patterns. So think of this as a newfound freedom. You've got options, baby!

With each project, I've given some basic sewing instructions to guide you through putting the pieces together. But I didn't get overly specific, because there is plenty of reference material out there for every sewing technique under the sun. Also, I figure if you're at the point in your sewing where you want to make your own patterns, you've probably got the basic skills down and have your own opinions and favorite tricks for bringing it all home. Still, I've got some tips and methods you may not be familiar with, so I'm going to share them with you now.

Seam Finishes

One of my biggest pet peeves in home sewing is the lack of importance placed on seam finishing. I find that most commercial sewing pattern instructions don't even mention finishing seams! This, in my opinion, is inexcusable. Seam finishing is vital, both functionally and aesthetically. If you don't finish the raw edges of your seam allowances, they can fray to the point that the seam actually comes apart. At the very least, unfinished seams look sloppy, and can cause lumps under your seams. This is the kind of thing that, once upon a time, made *home sewing* a dirty word. It's not difficult or time-consuming to finish your edges, and the professional-quality results are well worth the effort. My top four personal fave finishes are as follows:

French Seam

Ooh la la! It sounds so haute couture, doesn't it? This is hands-down my favorite because it looks even better than store-bought garments (which generally have serged edges). French seams are very clean and minimal but not difficult at all. The only catch is that you can only use them on straight (or slightly curved) seams, but if you think about it, most common seams (with the exception of armholes) fit into this category. I teach French seams to my beginner sewing students in their first project, the wrap skirt, so there's no reason why you can't do it, too. Here's how:

First, pin your seam together with *wrong sides facing*. Yes, I did mean to say wrong sides facing! I know it's crazy, but just have a little faith in me. Stitch the seam at ¼". (Note: If your total SA is only ½", stitch this first seam at a *scant* ¼". If you've got ⅝" SA, just make a normal ¼" seam.) Press the seam open, and trim the edges if they got a little hairy or wide at points. Then flip the seam, so that your right sides are now together and the raw edges are enclosed inside what will be the seam. Stitch again at ¼" (if you have ½" SA) or ⅜" (for ⅝" SA) and press to one side. Isn't that lovely?

Mock-French Seam Finish

This one is second on my list, because it looks nearly as good as my dear Frenchie. Sometime I forget that I wanted to make a French seam, and I've already made a **plain seam**, or else gathering or curves prevent me from doing it. The mock-French finish (like most seam finishes) is done *after* sewing a regular old plain seam. All you need to do is press the seam open, and then fold the raw edges in toward the center of the seam, so that they meet at the stitch line, and press again. Now bring the two folded edges together, pin, and edgestitch to close it up. Easy peasy, and good lookin' to boot.

Overedge Zigzag Finish

This is my third choice, because it works fine, but it's not as attractive as the first two. (Gosh, I'm starting to sound pretty shallow, aren't I?) The overedge zigzag is like the home version of serging, if you don't have a **serger**. Simply set your machine to a somewhat wide and short zigzag stitch (about 2–3mm wide, and 1–2mm long; experiment with a scrap of your fabric to see what works best). You can zigzag both SAs together, or do them individually, but just stitch along the raw edge, close enough that the needle goes off it on one side, wrapping the thread around the edge almost like a serger does. If your fabric is very thin, I'd recommend stitching both layers together and working close to, but not over, the edge.

FLAT-FELLED SEAM

I'm also a fan of flat-felled seams, which I suggested for the Rosie Skirt. These are the ones you see on the inseams of jeans, and they are very durable. To make a flat-felled seam, put wrong sides together and sew a (backwards) plain seam. Press it open, then to one side, and trim the bottom SA to half the size of the other. Fold the longer one over the shorter one, so the shorty is sandwiched inside, and pin against the body of the garment. Topstitch close to the fold.

Finishing Openings

There are plenty of options for finishing straight edges, or hems. My default is the double-turned ½" hem, accomplished by turning under ½" twice, and stitching close to the first fold. But curved openings, like waistlines, necklines and armholes (for sleeveless garments), require special treatment. You can't just finish these with a double-turned hem, because the circumference at the raw edge is so much smaller than the circumference even ½" in from the edge. In woven garments, my two favorite ways to finish these curved openings are bias facings and bias bindings. For knits, I like a folded band. I'll explain how to achieve each of these techniques.

BIAS FACINGS

Bias facings are how I prefer to finish the waistline of a skirt or pant with no waistband. Bias is the diagonal grain of fabric, at 45°, halfway between the straight grain and the cross grain. When the bias grain is used, pieces have more stretch and flexibility than if they were cut on the straight or cross grain. So bias tape can bend around even tight curves and still lay flat. You can cut strips of self-fabric (or contrast) bias yourself, or use premade single-fold bias tape. There are advantages to both. Making your own is a little time-consuming, and pressing the folds can be tricky. It uses up a lot of fabric, but you can choose whatever fabric and width you like, so

your options are wide open. Premade bias tape is limited in colors and sizes, and usually a poly/cotton blend, but it is convenient. Try both, and your favorite will probably alternate, depending on your project.

If you are cutting your own strips, they'll need to be twice as wide as your finished facing. Press both edges under to meet at the center, which will bring it to its finished width. Premade single-fold bias tape is usually ½" wide, and this works well around any curve. I wouldn't recommend trying a bias facing much wider than 1" (finished) on any but the slightest curve. To sew a bias facing, lay the tape, right sides together, with its raw edge even with the garment edge, and pin. Stitch inside the crease (for premade bias) or at ¼" from the edge. Flip the tape to the inside of the garment, so that the fold is on the seam, wrong sides together, and stitch again, close to the inner folded edge of the tape. From the right side of the garment, only this final stitch line will be visible.

BIAS BINDINGS

Bias bindings work well for necklines, especially where a tie-neck detail is used, as the binding can continue off the neck edge and become the ties. Again, you can use premade tape or make it yourself, but for binding you'll want double-fold tape. This just means it's folded again down the lengthwise center of the tape. A binding will show from the right side of the garment, so you'll definitely want to find a good match or contrast (or use self).

To sew a binding, open up one edge of your tape and lay it (right-side down) on the *wrong* side of your garment, edge to edge. Stitch inside the crease. Fold the tape up and around the garment edge, so that the edge is sandwiched in between both sides of the tape, and the tape is visible on the wrong side *and* the right side of your garment. Stitch again from the right side, close to the inner folded edge of the tape.

T-SHIRT NECKBANDS

For openings like a neckline or armhole in a knit, you'll need a finish that stretches. The classic T-shirt neck is a folded band of fine ribbing. It's pretty near impossible to find ribbing that matches your fabric, but for most knits a band of self will work just fine. Cut the band on the cross grain, twice as wide as your desired finished band, plus two times the SA. So for a ½" neckband, I would cut a 1½" wide strip (½" doubled equals 1", plus ¼" SA x 2). To determine the length of the band, measure the neckline or area it will be sewn onto, and subtract 10 percent. Add 1" SA (½" at each end). To sew the band, seam the short ends to form a loop. Fold the band in half down the entire length of it and press. It's helpful to stitch the two raw edges together at this point with an overedge zigzag. Then pin the band, right sides together, onto the neckline of the shirt, aligning the raw edges, and stitch using a stretch stitch or tiny zigzag. Flip the band up and press if necessary.

Stretch Stitching

While we're on the subject of sewing with knits, don't forget that knits should always be sewn with some kind of stretch stitch. You will definitely benefit from testing out some different stitches on a scrap of your fabric to see what works best. There are so many kinds of knits, and they all behave differently, so what works well on one may not for another. A straight stretch stitch, if your machine has it (most modern ones do; they are usually activated by setting the stitch length to "S.S.", but check your manual to be sure), works great on seams, but I find it's not the best for hemming, as it can stretch the hem out. A short and narrow zigzag (1.5–2mm in width and length) works well, and sometimes even better than a "real" stretch stitch. Experiment and see what gives the best effect for your project and fabric. It's also worth mentioning that most knits will not unravel, so I never finish my inside SAs, and I often even leave my hems and cuffs raw-edged because I like the clean look of it. After all, you are now the master of your designs, so every detail choice is up to you!

Blind Hemming

Topstitching was once considered a very *casual* treatment, and most clothing was hemmed by hand with a blind stitch, but now most of what we wear sports a topstitched hem. Nevertheless, nearly every

sewing machine I've seen, vintage or modern, has a blind hem stitch, and yet I find most people have no idea that such a thing even exists, much less that their very own machine can do it. It looks like a few straight stitches, then one zig and zag (see diagram). Check your machine now; I'll bet you have it! A blind hem is a beautiful way to finish the edge of dressier garments, like tailored pants, coats, or fancy dresses.

To do a blind hem on the machine: Turn up ½", and then ¾" to 1" or so, and press. Pin from the inside, with pins placed vertically and ⅜" down from the upper fold. Flip the folded and pinned hem toward the right side of the garment, so that from the wrong side, a small ¼" lip of the upper fold peeks out (see diagram). You will be stitching on this lip, with only the tips of the zigzags reaching over to catch *one or two threads* of the fold (which is the only time the stitching goes through to the right side of the garment).

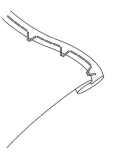

wrong side of hem while stitching

When you are done, unflip the folded hem, and you should see only the tiniest dots of stitches (where the zigzag pricked the fold) on the right side. Keep practicing on scraps until you get it down; it's really not difficult once you get the hang of it.

finished hem from right side

Invisible Zip

Now that you've mastered the blind hem, how about my other favorite hidden gem: the **invisible zipper**! I use these on dresses, and skirts and pants with no waistband, because they are so minimal. Honestly, ever since I learned how to insert an invisible zipper, I've never used a regular one! The only time I would consider going back is if I needed a separating zipper, like for a jacket, because invisibles have to be closed at the bottom.

To sew an invisible zipper, you need to get yourself an invisible zipper *foot*. I know, you think you have it already, because your sewing machine came with ten different feet, and at least one is called a zipper foot, so you must have it, right? Nope. I have yet to see a machine come with its own invisible zipper foot; don't ask me why. The ones most commonly available are inexpensive and plastic, and come with several shanks, so they should fit any home machine. Also, invisible zips *must* be inserted into a seam. This usually isn't a problem, but just be aware that if you're planning for a Center Back invisible zipper, you must have a Center Back seam. I usually put them at the side seam, so it's rarely an issue.

The seam where you'll be inserting the zipper must be completely open (unsewn). Unzip your zipper, and from the back, press (with your iron on low/synthetic or you'll melt the nylon zipper) the tape open where the teeth are curled back, so that they are pushed to the front and the tape appears flat, with no teeth visible. You will only be able to press the teeth open up to about ¼" from the pull at the bottom; don't worry, as this is normal. Once you've done this, don't zip the zipper back up until it's stitched in place, or you'll undo your pressing. Now lay one side of the zipper, facedown, onto the right side of your garment, with the toothless edge of the tape aligned with the raw edge of your seam (see diagram). Pin in place, and stitch right next to the teeth, where you pressed the zipper tape open. The zipper foot will help guide the needle exactly into the right place. Stitch from the top down toward the zipper pull, and stop when you are about ¼" from it, just as you did with the iron. You can't get much closer than this, so don't force it. Repeat the process, mirror-imaged, for the other side, but before you sew, just check that the zipper is placed correctly, both sides are even at the top edge, and nothing is twisted. When both sides are stitched,

zip up the zipper and change to your regular zipper foot, the one that came with your machine. Use this to sew the remaining portion of your seam, starting from the bottom. The foot will allow you to sew right up to the bottom end of your zipper seams. Aim to meet these seams exactly (don't overlap), and then backstitch. It may look a little wonky from the wrong side, but give the entire seam a good press and check it from the right side. Nine times out of ten it's exactly as it should be: invisible!

With these tips, plus your own arsenal of techniques, you should be able to handle sewing all of the projects in this book, even with my minimal instructions. I'm like a mama bird trying to push her babies out of the nest, and I have no doubt you can fly just fine on your own.

Glossary

Baste (or **basting**) A type of stitching in which a longer stitch length is used (usually the longest setting on the machine, or 4mm) to temporarily hold a seam for fitting or other purposes. The longer stitches allow basting to be ripped out easily

Bias The diagonal grain line at 45° from straight grain. Bias has more stretch and flexibility than straight or cross grain, and edges cut on the bias will not unravel

Bias tape A narrow piece of woven fabric cut on the bias and used as a trim for binding or facing, particularly on curves

Binding A technique used to finish raw edges by wrapping a thin strip of fabric (often bias tape) over the edge and topstitching

Blind hem A technique for hemming fine garments where the stitching is barely visible from the right side of the garment, done by hand or machine

Bodice The part of a dress or shirt that covers the torso; usually there will be a front and a back bodice

Center Back (CB) The invisible line down the center back side of a body. Most patterns for the backs of garments will be based around this line

Center Front (CF) The invisible line down the center front side of a body. Most patterns for the fronts of garments will be based around this line

Contrast Fabric that is different from the rest of the garment; often used as a styling element for smaller pattern pieces, such as collars, cuffs, and yokes

Crew neck A fairly high, traditional neckline, as seen on most classic T-shirts and sweaters

Cross grain The grain that runs perpendicular to, or 90° from, the straight grain

Curve rule or ruler The general name for the group of tools used to draw curves; includes hip curves and French curves

Cut-and-sew knits Garments made from knit fabric by cutting pieces out and sewing them together, as opposed to sweaters, which are knit in one (or very few) piece(s)

Dart A V-shaped wedge of fabric that will be seamed to allow three-dimensional shaping of a garment

Design elements The choices made by the designer, which add up to a complete design. Examples include silhouette, fit, fabrication, details, finishing, and color

Drape The quality of how a fabric hangs and moves on the body

Draping One of two methods of patternmaking, in which patterns are developed by hanging fabric (usually muslin) on a dress form

Dress form Also just called a "form"; a headless mannequin used for draping and fitting garments

Dressmaker's carbon paper A type of carbon paper for use on fabric, that washes out. Used for transferring markings from pattern to cloth, or pattern to pattern

Dropped waist A waistline that falls below the true waist

Ease The amount of space between the garment and the wearer that is built into the pattern in advance

Edgestitch A type of topstitching done very close ($1/16$–$1/8$") to an edge or seam

Empire waist A waistline above the true waist; often just below the bust

Facing A technique for finishing necklines, armholes, and waists with a strip of self-fabric or bias tape seamed to the inside edge of a garment; usually invisible from the right side

Flare Fullness added to a pattern so that it hangs or stands away from the body

Flat-felled seam A type of seam in which the seam allowances are folded under and top-stitched from the right side, commonly used on the inseam of jeans

Flat pattern One of two methods of pattern-making, and the kind used in this book, in which patterns are drafted flat on paper, using body measurements

French curve A tool used as a guide for drawing smooth curves

French seam A type of seam in which the raw edges are completely encased inside the seam allowance

Functional ease Extra room added to a pattern to allow for comfort and movement of the body

Gather To compress the edge of a longer piece of fabric so that it can be sewn to a shorter piece, as in a ruffle

Grading Increasing or decreasing the size of a pattern to fit a range of body sizes

Grain The direction in which a pattern piece is cut from the fabric, in reference to the selvage. The three grains are straight/lengthwise grain, cross grain, and bias

Grain line The line drawn on every pattern piece to indicate which way to lay the pattern in cutting. The line should always be parallel to the selvage of the fabric

Hard pattern A pattern made from oak tag or other heavy paper, which is used by placing weights on top and tracing around it, rather than pinning through it. Hard patterns are much more durable than soft tissue or paper patterns

High shoulder point (HSP) The point where shoulder meets neck, used as a reference point for length of garments

Hip curve A tool used in patternmaking as a guide for drawing smooth curves. Designed to approximate curves commonly used in patterns

inseam The seam that runs down the inner leg of pants

Invisible zipper A type of zipper that has the teeth on the back and doesn't show from the right side of the garment

Jersey A fine knit fabric most commonly used for T-shirts, with the stitch pattern of knit on the front and purl on the back. Same as stockinette stitch in hand knitting

Kick pleat A small pleat, usually placed at the CB hem of a skirt or dress, to allow for more movement, especially in a slim silhouette

Knit One of the two basic methods of fabric construction, in which one continuous yarn runs back and forth (or round and round in a tube) horizontally, each row looping and interlocking with the previous row

Lengthwise grain Also known as "straight grain," this is the direction parallel to the selvage in a piece of fabric. The grain line on a pattern should always be placed in this direction for cutting

Mock-French seam finish A way to finish the raw edges of a seam allowance after a plain seam has already been sewn, by tucking the raw edges in toward the center of seam, and re-stitching. Looks almost like the French seam

Muslin An inexpensive, undyed cotton fabric, used for draping or for test garments. Also, the name of such test garments, i.e., prototypes

Neck drop The distance from high shoulder point to the bottom of neckline, both in front and back

Negative ease Used in knit fabrics only, the difference between the size of the pattern and the body measurements, when the pattern is actually smaller than the body

Notch A mark, cut out on the edge of a pattern piece, to indicate a dart, where to match two separate pattern pieces, where a pattern will meet an intersecting seam, or front versus back

Oak tag A heavy paper used for making patterns in the industry

Obtuse angle An angle greater than 90°

Overedge zigzag A treatment commonly used to finish the edges of seam allowances, mimicking the function of a serger. It is a regular zigzag stitch used over the raw edge of the seam allowance.

Perpendicular At an angle of exactly 90°, which is also called a *right angle*

Plain seam The most basic and common type of seam, where two pieces are stitched together with the right sides facing each other

Pleat A device used for style or fit in which fabric is folded under itself and stitched across

Princess seam A traditional curved seam placement extending from armhole to hemline

Prototype Also called a *muslin;* the first sample made to test the fit of a new pattern

Pushpins The thumbtacks with the large "knobs" of either plastic or metal. Used for transferring lines from one pattern piece to another

Quadrant One-quarter of the body. Most patterns are made for either half of the front or half of the back, which equals one quarter

Recovery The ability of a fabric (usually knit) to return to its original size and shape after being stretched

Rib A knit fabric with a repeating pattern of knits and purls, making for a high degree of stretch and recovery

Right angle A 90° angle

Rise The seam in pants that runs from Center Front to Center Back between the legs, sometimes inelegantly called the *crotch seam*

Rubbing off The technique of obtaining a pattern from a finished garment

Seam allowance (SA) The extra width, usually ½" or 5/8", added beyond the seam line to all patterns for sewing

Seam finish Any of several various methods used to prevent the raw edges of seam allowances from unraveling, such as overedge zigzag, French seams, or mock-French finish

Seam line The line on a pattern exactly where the seam will be sewn

Self Same fabric as the rest of the garment. Or, if more than one fabric is used, the primary one (as opposed to contrast)

Selvage The finished edge that runs the length of most woven fabrics; used to designate straight or lengthwise grain

Serger A machine that finishes seams by wrapping multiple threads over the edges. Commonly used on commercial garments but also by many serious home sewers. Also called an *overlock* or *merrow* machine. (The stitch itself is called *serging)*

Shirring Slight gathering used as a style or fit device

Shoulder seam The seam line that runs along the shoulder, from neckline to armhole

Shoulder slope The angle given to a shoulder seam to reflect the shoulder angle of the wearer

Side seam The seam line that runs vertically down each side of the body, from underarm to hem

Silhouette The outer lines of a garment, which determine the overall shape

Slash and spread A technique used to add fullness or flare to a pattern by cutting it apart and spreading the pieces to enlarge

Sleeve cap The bell-shaped, curved top part of a sleeve pattern, extending from the underarm to the top of the shoulder

Slit An opening, usually at the bottom of a shirt, pant, or skirt side seam, where the seam is left partially unstitched for either decorative or functional purposes

Sloper A basic pattern piece, usually without seam allowance, used as a foundation for drafting fancier styles

Spandex The generic name for a synthetic fiber added to both knit and woven fabrics to increase stretch and recovery. Also known by its brand name, Lycra

Square Perpendicular, or 90°

Stay-stitch To stitch a raw edge, on or just outside of the seam line, before it is sewn to another piece, to prevent it from stretching out. Often used on curves or corners

Straight grain Also known as *lengthwise grain*, this is the direction parallel to the selvage in a piece of fabric. The grain line on a pattern should always be placed in this direction for cutting

Stretch stitch A stitch found on most modern sewing machines that makes a seam that will stretch, made by sewing two stitches forward and then one stitch backward

Stretch wovens Any woven fabric that has spandex added, to increase stretch and aid recovery

Style In clothing design, this term is used to describe one garment as opposed to another

Stylistic ease The type of ease added for aesthetic purposes, as opposed to fit or function

Sweep The measurement for the full circumference of the hem on a skirt or dress

Tailor's chalk or wax Small square chunks of chalk or wax used for temporarily marking on fabric. The marks come out with water, steam, or washing

Tissue jersey A very finely knit fabric that is almost sheer

Topstitch To stitch from the right side of the garment, often decoratively with heavier or contrasting thread

Tracing wheel A tool used by patternmakers, with needle points extending from the wheel, to transfer a line from one pattern piece to another by poking holes through the paper

True To check that all pattern pieces that will be seamed together are equal in length, that corners where seams will intersect are right angles, and that obtuse angles are blended into curves

True waist The smallest part of the waist, just below the ribcage

Tuck A styling or fitting device in which fabric is folded and then stitched along the fold so that it stands away from garment. Very small tucks are called pintucks

Underarm seam The seam line that runs the length of the underside of a sleeve, from underarm to inner wrist

Warp In woven fabrics, the yarns that run the lengthwise direction, which are usually heavier and stronger than the weft

Weft In woven fabrics, the yarns that run across the fabric, usually lighter-weight and less strong than the warp

Woven A fabric construction using two sets of yarns on the loom: the warp and the weft. The warp yarns, which run the length of the weave, are usually heavier and stronger. The weft yarns, which run back and forth across, alternating over and under each individual warp yarn, are generally lighter and not as strong

Yoke A horizontal seam line added for styling or fitting purposes to the top of a shirt, pant, or skirt. The pattern piece is often cut from contrast fabric

RESOURCE GUIDE

The following is a partial list of suggested retailers that stock the materials needed to create your own projects, inspired by those in this book. Some of these businesses I have patronized; others I haven't. I prefer to use only natural fibers in my designs, and organic ones when possible. I've also included a few of my favorite sewing books for reference.

Fabrics

Support your local independent fabric store! These are my own favorites in New York, as well as the shops I can't wait to check out the next time I'm in your neck of the woods:

BOLT FABRIC BOUTIQUE
2136 NE Alberta St.
Portland, OR 97211
www.boltfabricboutique.com
503-287-BOLT

BROOKLYN GENERAL STORE
128 Union Street
Brooklyn, NY 11231
www.brooklyngeneral.com
718-237-7753

CRAFT-O-RAMA
3100 S. Congress Ave., #3B
Austin, TX 78704
www.austincraftorama.com
512-707-2405

DIGS
310 Division Street South
Northfield, MN 55057
www.shopdigs.com
507-664-9140

METRO TEXTILE CORP.
265 West 37th Street, Suite 908
New York, NY 10018
metrotextile.blogspot.com
212-209-0004

P & S FABRICS
360 Broadway
New York, NY 10013
212-226-1534

SEWING ARTS CENTER
3330 Pico Blvd
Santa Monica, CA 90405
310-450-4300
www.sewingartscenter.com

SPOOL
1912 South Street
Philadelphia, PA 19146
www.spoolsewing.com
215-545-0755

STITCHES
711 East Pike Street
Seattle, WA 98122
206-709-0707
www.stitchesseattle.com

URBAN BURP
170 Columbus Avenue, Suite 110
San Francisco, CA 94133
415-399-8761
www.urbanburp.com

These online sources are great when you can't find what you want locally:

BAMBOO FABRIC STORE
www.bamboofabricstore.com
732-835-9326

CRYBABYS BOUTIQUE
www.crybabysboutique.com
714-527-2927

JO-ANN FABRIC AND CRAFT STORES
Visit www.joann.com to find a store in your area.
888-739-4120

NEAR SEA NATURALS
www.nearseanaturals.com
877-573-2913

REPRODEPOT
www.reprodepot.com

SEWZANNE'S FABRICS
www.sewzannesfabrics.com
888-620-8382

SUPER BUZZY
www.superbuzzy.com
805-644-4143

Notions and Sewing Supplies

CLOTILDE
www.clotilde.com
800-545-4002

NANCY'S NOTIONS
www.nancysnotions.com
800-833-0690

Patternmaking Supplies

ALBERT ZOLL, INC.
744 South 4th Street
Philadelphia, PA 19147
www.albertzoll.com
888-922-0589

ATLAS LEVY SEWING MACHINE CO.
722 S. Spring St.
Los Angeles, CA 90014
www.atlaslevy.com
800-216-9128

B. BLACK & SONS
548 South Los Angeles Street
Los Angeles, CA 90013
www.bblackandsons.com
800-433-1546

SEW TRUE
447 West 36th Street
New York, NY 10018
www.sewtrue.com
800-Sew-True

STEINLAUF AND STOLLER
239 West 39th Street
New York, NY 10018
www.steinlaufandstoller.com
877-869-0321

REFERENCES

Books

Jansdotter, Lotta. *Simple Sewing.*
San Francisco: Chronicle, 2007
>*I love the projects in this book and find
it to be a perfect lesson plan for beginner
stitchers.*

Karol, Amy. *Bend-the-Rules Sewing.* New York:
Potter Craft, 2007
>*Amy's style is so unique and fun, and
I adore her no-nonsense approach
to sewing.*

Mullin, Wendy. *Sew U.* New York: Bulfinch,
2006
———. *Sew U Home Stretch.* New York: Little,
Brown & Co., 2008
>*These two are must-haves for those who
want to sew their own clothing. Space
didn't permit me to get into the details of
how to sew the projects in this book, but
Wendy's books will tell you all you need
to know about garment construction.*

Reader's Digest Complete Guide to Sewing.
New York: Reader's Digest, 1976
>*This was my college textbook and it's
been my go-to sewing reference book
ever since. I believe there were later
editions but this is the one I have, and
I especially love the 70's projects in the
back!*

Online Sewing Reference and Articles

Threads magazine: www.taunton.com/
threads
>*I find the articles and videos on this site
endlessly helpful and comprehensive. It's
a great reference for techniques like "How
to sew a fly zipper".*

Burda Style: www.burdastyle.com
>*This online community contains a wealth
of information, like open-source patterns,
project galleries, articles and tutorials.*

Measurement Conversion Chart

Inches to Millimeters and Centimeters
(inches x 2.54 = centimeters)
(yards x 0.9144 = meters)

1/16" = 1.6mm	5 3/8" = 13.5cm	15 1/2" = 39.5cm	33" = 84cm	59" = 150cm	86" = 218.5cm
1/8" = 3mm	5 3/4" = 14.5cm	16" = 40.5cm	34" = 86cm	60" = 152.5cm	87" = 221cm
3/16" = 4.8mm	6" = 15cm	16 1/2" = 42cm	35 1/2" = 90cm	61" = 155cm	88" = 223.5cm
1/4" = 6mm	6 1/2" = 16.5cm	17" = 43cm	36" = 91cm	62" = 157.5cm	89" = 226cm
3/8" = 9.5mm	6 3/4" = 17cm	17 1/2" = 44.5cm	37" = 94cm	63" = 160cm	90" = 229cm
1/2" = 13mm	7" = 18cm	18" = 45.5cm	38" = 96.5cm	64" = 163cm	91" = 231cm
5/8" = 16mm	7 1/4" = 18.5cm	18 3/4" = 47.5cm	39" = 99cm	65" = 165cm	92" = 234cm
3/4" = 2cm	7 1/2" = 19cm	19" = 48.5cm	40" = 101.5cm	66" = 167cm	93" = 236cm
7/8" = 2.2cm	8" = 20.5cm	19 1/2" = 49.5cm	41" = 104cm	67" = 170cm	94" = 239cm
1" = 2.5cm	8 1/4" = 21cm	19 3/4" = 50cm	41 1/2" = 105.5cm	68" = 172.5cm	95" = 241cm
1 1/4" = 3cm	8 1/2" = 21.5cm	20" = 51cm	42" = 106.5cm	69" = 175cm	96" = 244cm
1 3/16" = 3cm	9" = 23cm	21" = 53.5cm	43" = 109cm	70" = 178cm	97" = 246cm
1 1/2" = 3.8cm	9 1/2" = 24cm	22" = 56cm	44" = 112cm	71" = 180cm	98" = 249cm
1 3/8" = 3.5cm	10" = 25.5cm	22 1/2" = 57cm	45" = 114cm	72" = 183cm	99" = 251.5cm
1 3/4" = 4.5cm	10 1/4" = 26cm	23" = 58.5cm	46" = 117cm	73" = 185cm	100" = 254cm
2" = 5cm	10 1/2" = 26.5cm	23 1/2" = 59.5cm	47" = 119cm	74" = 188cm	
2 1/4" = 5.5cm	11" = 28cm	24" = 61cm	48" = 122cm	75" = 190.5cm	
2 1/2" = 6.5cm	11 1/4" = 28.5cm	25" = 63.5cm	49" = 124.5cm	76" = 193cm	
3" = 7.5cm	12" = 30.5cm	26" = 66cm	50" = 127cm	77" = 195.5cm	
3 3/8" = 8.5cm	12 1/2" = 32cm	27 1/2" = 70cm	51" = 129.5cm	78" = 198cm	
3 1/2" = 9cm	13" = 33cm	28" = 71cm	52" = 132cm	79" = 200.5cm	
4" = 10cm	13 1/4" = 33.5cm	28 1/2" = 72cm	53" = 134.5cm	80" = 203cm	
4 1/2" = 11.5cm	13 1/2" = 34.5cm	29" = 74cm	54" = 137cm	81" = 206cm	
4 1/4" = 11cm	14" = 35.5cm	30" = 76cm	55" = 140cm	82" = 208cm	
4 3/4" = 12cm	14 1/2" = 37cm	31" = 79cm	56" = 142cm	83" = 211cm	
5" = 12.5cm	15" = 38cm	32" = 81cm	57" = 145cm	84" = 213cm	
5 1/2" = 14cm	15 1/4" = 38.5cm	32 1/2" = 82.5cm	58" = 147cm	85" = 216cm	

Index